NEAR-DEATH
EXPERIENCES
EXAMINED

Also from the Author

Et si on parlait des miracles... [And if we spoke of miracles...], 2nd edition
Paris: Presses de la Renaissance, 2004

Lourdes : des miracles pour notre guérison [Lourdes: miracles for healing]
Paris: Presses de la Renaissance, 2008

*Le témoignage incroyable d'un pèlerin, René Le Ménager, à Lourdes il y a
cent ans* [The incredible testimony of a pilgrim, René Le Ménager, in
Lourdes one hundred years ago]
Biarritz: Atlantica, 2008

*Une nouvelle approche biomédicale des maladies chroniques : l'endothérapie
multivalente* (avec le Dr Michel Geffard, directeur de recherche à l'INSERM)
[A new biomedical approach to chronic illness: multivalent nanotherapy,
(with Dr. Michel Geffard, INSERM Research Director)], 2nd edition
Paris: François-Xavier de Guibert, 2003

Publication Director

Être chrétien aujourd'hui dans sa pratique médicale [To be a Christian
today in one's medical practice], Conference Proceedings
Plans-Sur-Bex, Switzerland: Parole et Silence/NDL, 2005

Être médecin et chrétien aujourd'hui [To be a physician and Christian],
Conference Proceedings
Plans-Sur-Bex, Switzerland: Parole et Silence/NDL, 2007

In Collaboration

Dictionnaire des miracles et de l'extraordinaire chrétiens [Dictionary of
Christian miracles and extraordinary phenomena]
Paris: Fayard, 2002

Lourdes de A à Z [Lourdes from A to Z]
Bruyères-le-Châtel : Nouvelle Cité/NDL, 2008

Merveilles de Lourdes : 150 histoires [Wonders of Lourdes: 150 stories]
Paris: Mame/Magnificat/NDL, 2008.

Enquête sur les miracles. Pour la nouvelle évangélisation [Investigation into
miracles]
Montrouge: Editions du Jubilé, 2015

NEAR-DEATH EXPERIENCES EXAMINED

DR. PATRICK THEILLIER

Preface by MARC AILLET

A Crossroad Book
The Crossroad Publishing Company
New York

The Crossroad Publishing Company
www.CrossroadPublishing.com
© 2017 by Patrick Theillier

© 2015, Groupe Artège
Éditions Artège
10, rue Mercoeur - 75011 Paris
9, espace Méditerranée - 66000 Perpignan
www.editionsartege.fr.

The Publisher has the right to enter into this Agreement and owns and can convey the rights granted to Crossroad. Publisher further represents and warrants that the Work contains no libelous or unlawful material; it does not infringe upon or violate any copyright, or other right or the privacy of others. The Publisher further represents and warrants that the Publisher has obtained valid written agreements from the Author of the Work and all individuals or entities who contributed copyrightable material to the Work, enabling the Publisher to grant the rights herein granted to Crossroad (including but not limited to the right to translate and publish the Work, in whole or in part, in the English language throughout the world in book and eBook form and in the advertising, publicity and promotion thereof). The Publisher shall absolve and hold Crossroad, and its licensees, successors, and assigns, harmless from any alleged breach, or breach, of its representations and warranties hereunder, including any claim(s) of copyright infringement of any illustrations, photographs, quotations or other copyrighted material contained in the Work licensed herein. The Publisher shall keep said permission agreement(s) in force during the term of this Agreement and shall not permit any alterations or termination thereof which would affect Crossroad's rights under this Agreement.

Every effort has been made to present accurately, trace, and acknowledge source material used in the English translation of this book. The Publisher apologizes for any errors or omissions that may remain and asks that any omissions be brought to their attention so that they may be corrected in future editions.

Title by Patrick Theillier
Cover design by George Foster
Book design by Tim Holtz

Library of Congress Cataloging-in-Publication Data available from the Library of Congress.

ISBN : 978-0-8245-2217-9

I wrote this book in the company of Mariam, "the little Arab."
She was canonized by Pope Francis on May 17, 2015,
when I completed its writing. I dedicate it to her.

For my parents, Marc and Liliane,
and for my parents-in-law, Paul and Colette, living beyond the veil.

For my grandchildren, all living here and now, blessed be God!
Jean-Baptiste, Élisabeth, Marie-Liesse, François, Félicité,
Pierre, Edmée, Albert, Rémi, Philomène, Basile, Grégoire,
Madeleine, Bernadette, Armand, Joséphine, Louis, Henri,
Gabrielle, Geneviève, Aminthe, Joseph, Marthe, Marie,
Augustin, Étienne, Jacques,
the two who are still in their mother's womb,
and those to come …

Contents

I was suffering, I was suffering without any tangible cause of this suffering. Some possess the gift of living without any doubt about who they are or about the world around them. As for me, I was filled with questions, and my frustration was equaled only by my thirst for understanding. Honestly, I dreamt of the day when I would finally convince myself—such a difficult task—that there is no birth without death, nor death without rebirth. Under this double condition, life can have meaning.

    —Gilbert Sinoué

      La nuit de Maritzburg (Maritzburg night)

I rubbed elbows with death for many years and still I don't know anything about it, except that it kept me away from those that I loved most. Are they waiting for me somewhere? I want to believe it, and I'm not afraid. Because if no one is waiting for us on the other side of time, if nothing will be there to receive us, we will not know and we won't suffer from not knowing. But on the contrary, if we are welcomed we will surely be graced with the most beautiful feast. In the hope of having such a meeting, I will prepare myself as if preparing for an eternal wedding.

    —Christian Signol

        Tout l'amour de nos pères (The total love of our fathers)

And so my life is safe,
and I will live to tell
what the LORD has done.
    —Psalm 118:17

I promise that today you will be with me in paradise.
    —Luke 23:43

Eternal life is to know you, the only true God.
    —John 17:3

I tell you for certain that you will see heaven open and
God's angels going up and coming down on the Son of Man.
    —John 1:51

I shall not die, I do but enter into Life!
    —Thérèse of Lisieux

Preface

Dr. Patrick Theillier knows supernatural phenomena well. As physician of the Lourdes Office of Medical Observations, this committed and engaged Catholic man worked for ten years to scientifically prove, with the help of skeptical physician teams, the humanly inexplicable nature of healings that occurred under Our Lady of Lourdes' intervention, all of which were subjected to his scrutiny. Many of his findings have allowed the church to recognize authentic miracles. An unexplained healing is considered a miracle when the appropriate ecclesial authority recognizes a sign, which manifests as God's loving wisdom in humankind, capable of fortifying the faith of Christian people.

In this work, Dr. Theillier focuses on what we commonly call in English "near-death experience," or NDE, and that we translate in French as "*expériences de mort imminente*," or EMI. A great number of testimonials have been gathered over decades, and there is an abundant collection of literature on the topic. Varied witnesses from all cultures, not necessarily convinced of an afterlife, accurately testify to the existence of these strange phenomena that occur at death's door; thus, one can today establish a relevant typology that one would not want to reject without investigation.

As a well-informed scientist, Dr. Theillier begins by establishing the credibility of the testimonials he has gathered. Then, he passes them through the sieve of modern scientific knowledge to determine their scientific objectivity. Using Judeo-Christian anthropological resources, he can better describe these experiences and establish their compatibility with the faith. If scripture indicates that no one can return from death without a miracle, as in the resurrection-reanimation of Lazarus (see John 11) where one can attest that the spiritual soul was distinctly separated from the body—"Lazarus has been dead four days, and there will be a bad smell" (John 11:39)—we can conclude that there are experiences not of a metaphysical death but approaching an afterlife.

This work, therefore, is an opportunity to present an apology for our time. We live in a secular society, as if God did not exist, where people are duly satisfied with a science and a technology that pretend to explain everything and to organize everything about life—the totalitarianism of technoscience—and we paradoxically clash with the inexplicable. Theoretical and practical atheism, as professed by modern secularism in the name of scientific and technical progress, facilitates irrationality in our so-called evolved societies: a surge in blind violence, the rise of radical Islam, the expansion of esotericism.

Even in Christian funeral ceremonies, we can see signs that some want to conceal the reality of death as a last bastion against the mightiness of science and reason. In fact, who has not heard, at any given time, the famous expression falsely attributed to Saint Augustine or to Charles Péguy, "Death is nothing at all." It is as if some want to freely exorcise the anxiety that death increasingly provokes today. If there is one thing that is incontestable, it is that death exists. These near-death experiences, which have been scrutinized by science and by the faith, can in fact open our peers' intelligence and hearts to the existence of life after death and, in the same way, make them available to the annunciation of Christ's death and resurrection.

Our faith in the Resurrection is a sure gift from God, a spiritual enlightenment that allows us to believe in Mystery revealed. We can say this not because we are bound by our senses or by reasoning, but precisely because God himself says, "You didn't discover this on your own. It was shown to you by my Father in heaven" (Matthew 16:17). However, the church has always recognized that we have needed credible evidence in order to receive the gift of faith. Through Jesus's authoritative preaching and his intimate prayer giving God the name of "Abba," that is, "Papa," Peter is predisposed to believe in the miracles that were carried out in man's favor. He gradually opens his intelligence and his heart to the gift of faith: "You are the Messiah, the Son of the living God" (Matthew 16:16). As Thomas Aquinas writes, if faith is a gift from none other than God revealing himself in man's heart, one must however "see that one must believe." It is what I earlier called "credible evidence."

The atheistic and rational world in which we are living today needs credible evidence to predispose humankind to the saving grace of faith!

We must not doubt that God, who knows how to adapt to human nature—his own creation—arouses new credible evidences. The Holy Shroud of Turin is of this magnitude. It has been the object of unprecedented multidisciplinary studies: science remains stumped in spite of the most advanced investigations of this enigma, which could help so-called scientific civilization reach toward faith and Mystery. When Simon Peter sees the shroud laying on the ground and the strips of rolled cloth in the place of the head, John declares, "when he saw it, he believed" (John 20:8). Peter sees the shroud and he believes in the Mystery of the Resurrection, because he did not yet understand "the Scriptures said Jesus would rise to life" (John 20:9). God revealing himself through his Word is the real cause of a beloved disciple's faith, but he is more likely to welcome this by noticing the collapsed shroud.

The same goes for NDEs. It is in the mystery of Christ resurrected that humankind, searching for a light to illuminate all existence, finds an answer to the ultimate question about death. The NDEs in turn give meaning to this luminosity by almost invariably offering a light at the end of a tunnel! Dr. Patrick Theillier knows how to reconcile science and religion, reason and faith. His whole approach points to an interest in these strange phenomena as "credible evidence," such that our contemporaries might open themselves to have faith in the mystery of Christ's death and resurrection, he who offered us eternal life. As an avid reader of the scripture, which he accesses through a careful reading of the Bible, Dr. Theillier knows how to enlighten us on his approach, step by step, with the help of the Word of God. Yet again we can rely on the statement from Blaise Pascal: "Submission of reason, greatness of reason!" In the face of the inexplicable, it is the greatness of reason to submit oneself to faith. Faith is not the attitude of one who capitulates to the inexplicable; it is the attitude of one who welcomes a higher revelation without which reason could not bear to go on its insatiable quest for truth. As Saint John Paul II writes in the frontispiece of the masterwork that is the encyclical *Fides et Ratio*:

> Faith and reason are like two wings on which the human spirit rises to the contemplation of truth; and God has placed in the human heart a desire to know the truth—in a word, to know himself—so that, by knowing and loving God, men and women may also come to the fullness of truth about themselves.[1]

Assuredly, Dr. Theillier's book is like a sprig of hope in a world closed off to transcendence and whose culture is characterized by an immanentistic humanism. As Pope Francis writes in his encyclical letter *Lumen fidei* ("The Light of Faith"):

> Only from God, from the future which comes from the risen Jesus, can our society find solid and lasting foundations. In this sense faith is linked to hope, for even if our dwelling place here below is wasting away, we have an eternal dwelling place which God has already prepared in Christ, in his body.[2]

May this work reach out to a great many of our contemporaries who struggle with the enigma and anguish of death. May it let Jesus resurrected pronounce for them the same words given to Thomas, the disbelieving apostle:

> Put your finger here and look at my hands! Put your hand into my side. Stop doubting and have faith…. Do you have faith because you have seen me? The people who have faith in me without seeing me are the ones who are really blessed! (John 20:27–29).

—Marc Aillet
    Bishop of Bayonne, Lescar, and Oloron
    June 29, 2015, for the solemnity of Saints Peter and Paul

—⟨∿⟩—

Introduction

Who hasn't dreamt of visiting the afterlife and to return from it to strengthen one's hope and to illuminate one's earthly existence?
—Michel Aupetit

As we begin this century, Western society prefers not to hear about death, expunging all that concerns it, even in the vocabulary. The word itself—"death"—has become taboo; we speak of "disappearance" or "end of life." Still, no matter what we do, and regardless of medical advances and human longevity, we very well know that we remain mortals and that we cannot resist asking the questions that are on everyone's heart: *Does something exist after life? Is death really the end of life? Does life really end with death?*

How would we know? What might help enlighten us? Philosophical writings on death are hardly convincing, and they do not teach us how to die. Religions, beginning with Christianity, have advanced serious arguments allowing us to believe that earthly existence does not end with death and that life continues, that we will rejoin those we loved in this life. We must nonetheless have faith or we risk believing, for a moment, that from death *no one has ever returned.*

Whether we believe in heaven or not, we are haunted with the question: Is there not, deep inside, always a glimmer of hope that death will not be the end of life? And if we had, after all, any clue that life is stronger than death, would it not be very good news for each one of us?

At each epoch in history, there have been signs that should not be ignored. For the last forty years we have had the primordial sign of those who allegedly have laid foot in the afterlife and returned in extremis. Can we believe them?

We understand that a sign comes from a heart-centered understanding, which is always accessible. We must seriously examine it, which is what I am proposing here.

This sign therefore comes from ordinary people, like you and me, who were pronounced clinically dead and who tell of having been in another world, a magnificent world, that they needed to leave to return to earth. From then on, they say they have experienced a kind of second birth: They do not see existence in the same way, their spirituality is reinforced, their love of others comes first, they are aware of the sacredness of life, they consider death as being part of life and therefore they are no longer scared of it.

This is what we call in English near-death experience, or NDE, since the 1975 publication of Raymond Moody's foremost book, *Life after Life,* which was translated into twenty-six languages. We owe him the phenomenon's popularization and intense media scrutiny. Today, NDEs have been translated in French as *expérience de mort imminente,* or EMI.

For those of us who have not had these experiences, are we not spontaneously drawn to believe that these phenomena are imaginary and that they are fabrications of eccentrics with fragile psyches or who are seeking attention? The problem lies in that we do not know if we can trust these remarkable experiences, since they challenge our conviction that no one can ever return from death. It is important to understand that these strange events at the edge of death seem to have always existed: they were recounted throughout history and in all civilizations. For about forty years now, thanks to resuscitation techniques and modern communication systems, they seem to be more frequently recounted and recognized. We might even say that the many justifiable NDEs surveyed and analyzed worldwide through different means, as well as the numerous works, studies, publications, and scientific colloquia devoted to the topic, urge us to not doubt their existence in this twenty-first century.[1] Still, we must investigate what they represent.

As unusual as they might seem, these experiences surely deserve our attention while still judging them objectively, much like we would do with any other bizarre occurrence. Herein lies the objective of this book.

Of course, let us not be naïve. A search on the Internet reveals all sorts of extravagant back-to-life stories that make us wonder if it is not another scheme of profiteers, especially those of the nebulous New Age. Books on the afterlife are amply displayed in bookstore windows and are classified in the "esotericism and paranormal" section. In this irrational world, many stories have been added to the mix and their shocking revelations add further speculation to what they proclaim.

Does this mean that we should close the doors on this tradition and abandon these findings to the esoteric world without searching any further?

We need to recognize that it is not easy to accept the existence of such complex events that are theoretically isolated, subjective, often ignored, or poorly perceived. This is especially true in light of an often too radical rationalism stemming from the still very scientific domain of classical science, as well as from a religious domain that is either too conservative (unable to separate itself from its own representations) or too progressive (tempted to close itself off from the scientifically correct ideas of the world).

It is a fact that a majority of scientists reject these events as somehow originating from a mental process. Thus, as surprising as it might seem, we will see that these events have resisted the most serious critiques, which in turn challenge the dogmatic notion that consciousness is a product of the brain.

Paradoxically, for Catholics who have faith in the eternal life in accordance with the Apostle's Creed ("I believe in the resurrection of the body and in life everlasting"), the general tendency is to also doubt the existence of these phenomena, which are mostly considered superfluous and difficult to integrate. It is true that they are not essential to the faith, but could they not be of great help in our secularized world where the existence of invisible things is problematic? Many Christians are no longer convinced that there is life after death and therefore see it as a vague eventuality.[2]

This book has no other purpose than to understand near-death experiences as objectively as possible, relative to science and faith; that is, Catholic faith, which is the only one I significantly understand.[3]

Thus, I would like to comfort those who believe as well as those who do not—we all need reassurance—in the hope that death most certainly does not have the last word.

I will therefore start by listing the facts, beginning with a number of texts and stories from those who have experienced NDEs. Then we will examine them under the microscope of science and the Christian religion, reflecting on what these stories have to offer both reason and faith, assuming that there is no opposition between the two. This topic is a perfect example of this.

I must let you know that I have not experienced such a phenomenon. Therefore, one might ask what makes me a legitimate spokesperson for this topic. It is in my roles as a physician as well as a Catholic that I wanted to develop a deeper understanding of this theme that contributes to the increasingly necessary dialogue between reason and faith, something I have already attempted in my other works.

It so happens that, as a young physician, I was duly impressed with Dr. Moody's book, finally discovering a colleague who ventured outside of the medical consensus, one that believes nothing exists outside of the "psychosomatic." This led me to reorient my practice toward a person-centered medicine—in the whole sense of the expression—and brought me to take on, at the end of my career, the permanent physician position of the Lourdes Office of Medical Observations, with the objective of authenticating the declarations of healings that could be of miraculous origins.

I noted many similarities between these near-death experiences and extraordinary phenomena such as miraculous healings, Marian apparitions, or events noted among mystics (recognized in certain cases, following long and serious observations, by the Catholic Church). I dedicate a chapter to it. In this light, I have also highlighted the passages from the scripture that sometimes strikingly correspond to the facts and I added reflections or various experiences that illustrate the subject.

I leave it to each of you to have your own opinion on the matter.

My friends, we want you to understand how it will be for those followers who have already died. Then you won't grieve over them and be like people who don't have any hope. We believe that Jesus died and was raised to life. We also believe that when God brings Jesus back again, he will bring with him all who had faith in Jesus before they died (1 Thessalonians 4:13–14).

"One Must No Longer Fear Death!"

This is the story of testimony that I recorded in Lourdes. Note the healing that occurred at the same time as the near-death experience, which is not a rare occurrence (see "Other Extraordinary Phenomena").

Mr. Michel Durant was born in 1933; he was the oldest of eleven children. Married and the father of two children, he was a sensible man who was engaged in various organizations and served as the deputy mayor of his town.

In 2003, Michel had a sudden attack of cholecystitis (a grave inflammation of the gallbladder) causing perforation of the bile duct and of the intestine, septicemia, infection at the base of the lungs, and, to top it all, pancreatitis that seriously complicated matters. It seemed everything that could go wrong did, necessitating an urgent and risky intervention.

In the course of this intervention, he suffered cardiac arrest and was pronounced clinically dead. At the same time, his young nephew, a Dominican, who was the son of his youngest sister and the eleventh of the family, was in Lourdes praying for his uncle; he specifically went to the pools to pray for his uncle's health. Amazingly, the resuscitating team managed to reanimate the heart, and in one day Michel was able to stand. With his health rapidly improving, he was able to return home after four weeks. After seven weeks, he went to see his surgeon, who received him, exclaiming, "Here's the miracle!"

I first heard this story from the nephew on October 6, 2004, during the pilgrimage of the Lourdes Rosary, on which I was the physician responsible for the Office of Medical Observations. I met his uncle on October 8, 2004, and then again in October 2006. Calmly, he told me that he was not claiming a miracle and that, after all, the physicians performed well, which was true. Nonetheless, he admitted, "I recognize that this healing was given to me by the Virgin. For one who is very Marian, this is a gracious gift." Then, as we continued to talk, he finally decided to disclose his experience of "clinical death":

> At some point, a door opened with a great light in front of me. It was not in a tunnel for me. I was alone, in a clear, calm, relaxing, indescribable state. I had a sense I was headed for something formidable, marvelous. How long did it last? I can't even tell. Time no longer existed. In any case, it was a very pleasant experience. It was a state of happiness, of well-being, of fullness. Everything was beautiful, everything was serene. It's inexplicable how good it felt! I lived through perfect grace. The worst part was coming back to the sad reality of being hooked up to all sorts of machines!
>
> There is much to reflect upon. Afterward, it took me a while to talk about it. I felt as if I were at a critical juncture; my spirit found itself in another part of my life. And then I told myself I needed to bear witness to this unexplainable healing and tell those who would hear my story. I needed to proclaim that there is something afterward; life on earth can no longer be the same. Everything is relative; life cannot be seen from the same angle. It makes one happy to have experienced it. It makes one want to say thank you; to pray in a spirit of praise and recognition rather than petition.
>
> There is no need to be depressed. If this is death, one must no longer fear it. When I am confronted with the death of someone I know and love, I will not see it as an end in itself. It seems I have already experienced it this way, perhaps so I could witness it in others.

A Fable

Twins in the belly of their mother:

"Say, do you believe we'll stay here a long time?"

"All the time, of course! It's way too nice here!"

"I don't know, but I have this feeling that there's something after this."

"Something after?"

"Yes, another life. In my opinion, we're here to become strong and to prepare ourselves for what comes next."

"But, wait, that's foolish. There is nothing after. What you're saying is silly. Why would you want to have something else outside of this space? What would life outside of the womb look like?"

"Well, there are many stories about 'the other side.' They say that 'over there,' there's plenty of light, lots of joy and emotions, thousands of things to experience. For instance, they say that 'over there' we will eat with our mouths."

"That's nonsense! We have the umbilical cord and that's what nourishes us, everyone knows! We don't feed ourselves through the mouth! And there's never been a revenant from this other life in which you believe. These are all stories from naïve people. Life simply ends at birth. That's how it is; we need to accept this."

"Well, I will have to disagree. For sure, I don't know exactly what life will look like after delivery and I can't prove anything. But I do believe in a life that will come after this. We will see our mom and she'll love us and take care of us.

"'Mom'? You mean you believe in 'mom'? Ah! And where is she?"

"Well, she's everywhere, you know that! She's here, everywhere around us. We are made from her and it's thanks to her that we exist. Without her, we wouldn't be here."

"That's absurd! I have never seen any 'mom.' She doesn't exist."

"I don't agree. That's your perspective! There are times, when everything is calm, we can hear her singing. We can feel her when she caresses our world. I am most certain that our real life will start after delivery."

What Is a Near-Death Experience?

Take away the supernatural, and what remains is the unnatural.
  —G. K. Chesterton

A "Classic" Near-Death Experience

Every near-death experience (NDE) is unique and personal but all have striking similarities. We will see a number of examples throughout this book. However, it seems useful to refer to pioneering NDE researcher Dr. Raymond Moody's first account, drawn from 150 testimonies and offered in his seminal book, *Life after Life*:

> A man is dying and, as he reaches the point of greatest physical distress, he hears himself pronounced dead by his doctor. He ... feels himself moving very rapidly through a long dark tunnel. After this, he suddenly finds himself outside of his own physical body, but still in the immediate physical environment, and he sees his own body from a distance, as though he is a spectator....
>
> After a while, he collects himself and becomes more accustomed to his odd condition. He notices that he still has a "body," but one of a very different nature and with very different powers from the physical body he has left behind. Soon ... others come to meet and to help him. He glimpses the spirits of relatives and friends who have already died, and a loving, warm spirit of a kind he has never encountered before—a being of light—appears before him. This being asks him a question, nonverbally, to make him evaluate his life and helps him along by showing him a panoramic, instantaneous playback of the major events of his life. At some point he finds himself approaching some sort of barrier or

border, apparently representing the limit between earthly life and the next life. Yet he finds that he must go back to the earth, that the time for his death has not yet come. At this point he resists, for by now he is taken up with his experiences in the afterlife and does not want to return. He is overwhelmed by intense feelings of joy, love, and peace. Despite his attitude, though, he somehow reunites with his physical body and lives.

Later he tries to tell others, but he has trouble doing so. In the first place, he can find no human words adequate to describe these unearthly episodes. He also finds that others scoff, so he stops telling other people. Still, the experience affects his life profoundly, especially his views about death and its relationship to life.[1]

Near-death experiences are not rare or isolated phenomena. In the United States, according to notable NDE researcher Kenneth Ring, there have been about 8 million accounts of people who have had these experiences (that is, 30 percent of people who have nearly died).[2] This would be equivalent to some 1.4 million people in France.[3] Today, we identify these people by the American neologism, "experiencer," which is translated in French as *expérienceur*.

In 1998, Jeffrey Long, a self-described man of science, created the Near Death Experience Research Foundation in the United States and its website to gather the greatest number of probable testimonies using a survey with some one hundred questions.[4] More than thirteen hundred people from every corner of the world, regardless of race or creed, responded to the survey in the first ten years. As Long says in his book *Evidence of the Afterlife: The Science of Near-Death Experiences*:

> That so many people are willing to share their NDEs with others speaks volumes about the power of these experiences in a person's life. Respondents describe their experiences in a variety of ways, calling them "unspeakable," "ineffable," "unforgettable," "beautiful beyond words," and so on. More than 95 percent of the respondents feel their NDE was "definitely real," while virtually all of the remaining respondents feel it was "probably real." Not

one respondent has said it was "definitely not real." Some say it was not only the most real thing to ever happen to them but also the best event of their lives.[5]

According to epidemiological studies, NDE testimonies may be more frequent among people under sixty years old. Children experience NDEs, especially those under four years of age (see "Second Testimony"). They do not know what death is; they are not culturally or religiously conditioned, and they certainly have not heard of NDEs. So even if we try to talk to them about these experiences, they would not understand.

Near-death experiences were reported during numerous situations, namely cardiac arrest (clinical death), hemorrhagic shock, traumatic brain injury or intracerebral hemorrhage, drowning, or asphyxia. Similar experiences can also occur during serious non-life-threatening illnesses, during final phases of illnesses, during a crucial moment in life (such as when a patient hears that he has been declared dead), or when a person senses she is in a fatal situation (such as just before a car or climbing accident). These are called "deathbed visions."

Only 20 to 30 percent of people who have nearly died undergo an NDE. One cannot predict who will be predisposed to an NDE when approaching death; there are no advance warnings. Thus NDEs present quite randomly. Children, the elderly, scientists, physicians, the religious—all have reported them. There is, in fact, no increase in reports among believers than among atheists.

It is impossible to voluntarily experience an NDE or to experimentally induce one in a patient, neither physically nor ethically. Finally, be aware that some experiences similar to NDEs have been reported in people who were not close to death or gravely ill. Dr. Raymond Moody speaks of "shared-death experience" or "empathic NDE" that happens at the moment of death of a loved one. Some people, such as Martin Restrepo, prisoner of the FARC in Colombia, have been able to have an NDE at a moment of great fear of death. Restrepo's life was completely upstaged by his experience.

In fact, NDEs are closely related to charismatic or mystical experiences. There is always a limit; we can associate them but we should not confound them.

The Different Phases of Near-Death Experience

Let us look into the different phases of near-death experience to which we will refer in later chapters of the book in order to illuminate certain scientific as well as religious points. These phases are potential without being obligatory, and they do not necessarily happen in a single order.

I have gathered nine:[6]

1. A "disembodiment" or sense of being out of body
2. A change in the body's state
3. The passage through a tunnel
4. Contact with other "spiritual beings"
5. Encounter with a "being of light"
6. A life review
7. A sense of peace and tranquility
8. The return
9. Repercussions on one's way of life

In the sections that follow, I refer to certain passages from *Embraced by the Light*, a book originally published in 1992 that I keep safely in my library.[7] The book's author, Betty J. Eadie, is the child of an Indian mother and an Irish-Scottish father. Betty bears all the marks of a difficult childhood: her parents divorced, she was placed in an orphanage, she was separated from her siblings, and her first marriage failed. She married again, to a man named Joe, with whom she had eleven children. A widow since 2011, she is the grandmother of fifteen grandchildren and seven great-grandchildren.

After an unfortunately strict Catholic education, Betty converted to the Church of Jesus Christ of Latter-Day Saints (Mormon faith), where she assumed some responsibilities after her NDE.

Betty "died" on November 18, 1973, at the age of thirty-one, following a surgical procedure (partial hysterectomy that led to a cataclysmic hemorrhage). She came back to life and recounted her story of the afterlife in a detailed and captivating way. It took her nineteen years and lots of encouragement, following many conferences she gave on the topic, before writing her book, therefore not everything she wrote can be taken literally—with time, there is a tendency to embellish or romanticize pleasant memories of the past.[8] Still, we cannot doubt her testimony; she certainly did not invent this. Note that I only rely on the material that corresponds to the different phases listed above. Additionally, it seems interesting to juxtapose these different steps with excerpts from the scriptures as signposts.

1. The "Disembodiment"

The disembodiment, which we also call out-of-body experience (OBE), is the subjective experience of a human being's exit from his body. It is usually the first step in the NDE (in about 45 percent of cases). Many of the testimonies concur: a person finds himself most often close to the ceiling of the resuscitation room calmly observing the doctors and nurses busying themselves around his body, changing the infusion bottles, and exchanging comments. They can eventually check the accuracy of behaviors and statements.

Here is how Betty describes her experience in chapter 4 of *Embraced by the Light*:

> I heard a soft buzzing sound in my head and continued to sink until I felt my body become still and lifeless. Then I felt a surge of energy. It was almost as if I felt a pop or release inside me, and my spirit was suddenly drawn out through my chest and pulled upward, as if by a giant magnet. My first impression was that I was free. There was nothing unnatural about the experience. I was above the bed, hovering near the ceiling. My sense of freedom was limitless and it seemed as if I had done this forever. I turned and saw a body lying on the bed. I was curious about who it was, and immediately I began descending toward it. Having worked as an LPN [licensed practical nurse], I knew well the appearance of a dead body, and as I got closer to the face I knew at once that it was lifeless. And then I recognized that it was my own. That was my body on the bed. I wasn't taken aback, and I wasn't frightened; I simply felt a kind of sympathy for it. It appeared younger and prettier than I remembered, and now it was dead. It was as if I had taken off a used garment and had put it aside forever, which was sad because it was still good—there

was still a lot of use left in it. I realized that I had never seen myself three-dimensionally before; I had only seen myself in the mirror, which is only a flat surface. But the eyes of the spirit see in more dimensions than the eyes of the mortal body. I saw my body from all directions at once—from in front, behind, and from the sides. I saw aspects to my features I had never known before, adding a wholeness, a completeness to my view. This may be why I didn't recognize myself at first.[9]

For Dr. Jeffrey Long:

We noted a number of NDEs where consciousness seemed to have left the body and distanced itself from the latter. For example, consider a patient who had cardiac arrest in the operating room; his consciousness left the body and went to the cafeteria where his family was. Everything was later verified; everything was precisely the same. It's fascinating, and we have a number of similar examples. And the details are never inaccurate. I would be very surprised if we found someone who reported false observations. The small percentage of discrete observations is often related to one or two details. Out-of-body observations, the reality of what these people see when they are unconscious, that is, in a clinical death, and the reality of what they see when they are at a distance from their body is one of the greatest proofs we have about the authenticity of NDEs.[10]

Classical science cannot even comprehend this kind of observation. As for theology, we will look at it in a later chapter, "Anthropological Approach" (see p. 79), through the lens of anthropology.

I know about one of Christ's followers who was taken up into the third heaven fourteen years ago. I don't know if the man was still in his body when it happened, but God certainly knows. As I said, only God really knows if this man was in his body at the time. But he was taken up into paradise, where he heard things that are too wonderful to tell (2 Corinthians 12:2–4).

2. A Change in the Body's State

Conscience and lucidity are reinforced by intense and generally positive emotions or feelings.

> My new body was weightless and extremely mobile, and I was fascinated by my new state of being. Although I had felt pain from the surgery only moments before, I now felt no discomfort at all. I was whole in every way—perfect. And I thought, "This is who I really am."[11]

At that moment, Betty thinks of her family and realizes that she can leave her room by going through walls. She can also travel to her home "at a tremendous speed," watch her family without being noticed, and instantaneously return to her hospital room where "I saw my body still lying on the bed about two and a half feet below me and slightly to my left."[12] The experiencer's body is therefore no longer material, solid, opaque, but there is nonetheless a body. What shall we call it? "Mystical" body, "spiritual" body, "splendid" body?

In esoteric circles, people speak of "subtle body" or "astral body," an intermediary between the physical body and the spirit. They describe an energetic or undulating nature, able to detach itself from the physical body and travel—what is called "astral travel"—and to come in contact with other "entities."

In any case, classical science is not open to discussing this kind of phenomenon. Can quantum physics perhaps imagine such a possibility?

> The disciples were afraid of the Jewish leaders, and on the evening of that same Sunday they locked themselves in a room. Suddenly, Jesus appeared in the middle of the group. He greeted them (John 20:19).

3. The Passage through a Tunnel

This stage consists (in most cases) of the passage through a tunnel at very high speed, ending up in an unknown place—a place that could be called nonterrestrial because it resembles nothing like earth and what we know of it. Hieronymus Bosch's *Ascent into the Empyrean* is a lovely example. Those who experience the passage say of Bosch's image, "That's it!"

Generally—for almost two-thirds of cases—at the end of the tunnel shimmers a white light; it is appealing, as bright as "a million suns," but it is not blinding. Let us look again at Betty's story (chapter 5, "The Tunnel"). She says that she finds herself "in the presence of enormous energy." She should be terrified but instead she has "a profoundly pleasant sense of well-being and calmness."[13]

> I felt a process of healing take place. Love filled this whirling, moving mass, and I sank more deeply into its warmth and blackness and rejoiced in my security and peace. I thought, "This must be where the valley of the shadow of death is." I had never felt greater tranquility in my life.[14]

People find themselves in a different time-space. They have the impression that they are entering another world, that they have access to understanding the universe in a particular way and to discovering celestial, spiritual kingdoms.

> Never again will night appear, and no one who lives there will ever need a lamp or the sun. The Lord God will be their light, and they will rule forever (Revelation 22:5).

4. Contact with Other "Spiritual Beings"

People who experience an NDE tell of encountering predeceased loved ones, mostly close relatives who were either known or unknown to them before the NDE. Sometimes they encounter spiritual beings. Shall we call them "people," "mystical beings," or "spirits"? In any case, they are not pure spirits: they are recognizable and they talk, for example. All testimonies concur.

> In this place I saw people that I knew had died. There were no words spoken, but it was as if I knew what they were thinking, and at the same time I knew that they knew what I was

thinking. I felt a peace that passed all understanding. It was a marvelous feeling. I felt exhilarated and felt I was one with everything.[15]

The poor man died, and angels took him to the place of honor next to Abraham.

The rich man also died and was buried. He went to hell and was suffering terribly. When he looked up and saw Abraham far off and Lazarus at his side (Luke 16:22–23).

5. Encounter with a "Being of Light"

People describe an ineffable encounter with a being of light from who emanates an infinite, unconditional love. Descriptions of these encounters are often the same: imagine a light filled with complete understanding and perfect love; the love that emanates from the light is unimaginable, indescribable.

A fifty-year-old woman, Fabienne, who suffered from a diabetic coma at age twelve, was believed dead, since she reentered her body at the morgue. She never forgot this experience. She admits, "I encountered a light that was all Love."

A young American soldier, George Ritchie, caught a fever during an intensive training and was believed dead. He recounts his discovery of the light source:[16]

[It was] He. He would be too bright to look at. For now I saw that it was not light but a Man who had entered the room, or rather, a Man made out of light, though this seemed no more possible to my mind than the incredible intensity of the brightness that made up His form.

The instant I perceived him, a command formed itself in my mind. "Stand up!" The words came from inside me, yet they had an authority my mere thoughts had never had. I got to my feet and as I did came the stupendous certainty: "You are in the presence of the Son of God...."

Above all, with that same mysterious inner certainty, I knew that this man loved me. Far more even than power, what emanated from this Presence was unconditional love. An astonishing love. A love beyond my wildest imagining....[17]

This meeting with the being of light seems to have the power to completely transform those who have this experience.

It could be an angelic encounter, but most testimonies concur that these are more likely divine encounters. In his two works, Dr. Moody offers a great number of testimonies about this light:

> Typically, at its first appearance this light is dim, but it rapidly gets brighter until it reaches an earthly brilliance.... Despite the light's unusual manifestation, however, not one person has expressed any doubt whatsoever that it was a being, a being of light. Not only that, it is a personal being. It has a definite personality. The love and the warmth which emanate from this being to the dying person are utterly beyond words.[18]

A testimony from Dr. Moody's *Life after Life*:

> I was trying to get to that light at the end, because I felt that it was Christ, and I was trying to reach that point. It was not a frightening experience. It was more or less a pleasant thing. For immediately, being a Christian, I had connected the light with Christ who said, "I am the light of the world." I said to myself, "If this is it, if I am to die, then I know who waits for me at the end, there in that light."[19]

In another of Dr. Moody's books, *The Light Beyond*, an experiencer says the following:

> I was in the light a long time. It seemed like a long time. I felt everyone loved me there. Everyone was happy. I feel that the light was God.[20]

As for Betty, here is what she says in her chapter 6, "In the Arms of Light":

I saw a pinpoint of light in the distance. The black mass around me began to take on more of the shape of a tunnel, and I felt myself traveling through it at an even greater speed, rushing toward the light. I was attracted to it.... As I approached it, I noticed the figure of a man standing in it, with the light radiating all around him. As I got closer the light became brilliant—brilliant beyond any description, far more brilliant than the sun—and I knew that no earthly eyes in their natural state could look upon this light without being destroyed. Only spiritual eyes could endure it— and appreciate it. As I drew closer, I began to stand upright.

I saw that the light immediately around him was golden, as if his whole body had a golden halo around it, and I could see that the golden halo burst out from around him and spread into a brilliant, magnificent whiteness that extended out for some distance. I felt his light blending into mine, literally, and I felt my light being drawn to his. It was as if there were two lamps in a room, both shining, their light merging together. It's hard to tell where one light ends and the other begins; they just become one light. Although his light was much brighter than my own, I was aware that my light, too, illuminated us. And as our lights merged, I felt as if I had stepped into his countenance, and I felt an utter explosion of love.

It was the most unconditional love I have ever felt, and as I saw his arms open to receive me I went to him and received his complete embrace and said over and over, "I'm home. I'm home. I'm finally home." I felt his enormous spirit and knew that I had always been a part of him.... There was no questioning who he was. I knew that He was my Savior, and friend, and God. He was Jesus Christ, who had always loved me, even when I thought he hated me. He was life itself, love itself, and his love gave me a fullness of joy, even to overflowing.[21]

Six days later Jesus took Peter and the brothers James and John with him. They went up on a very high mountain where they could be alone. There in front of the disciples, Jesus was completely changed. His face was shining like the sun, and his clothes became white as light (Matthew 17:1–2).

6. The Life Review

At this point, the dying person often witnesses a kind of movie of his life (or fragments of his existence) pass by him in a moment. The being of light seems to know everything about him and asks—with great tenderness and loving intention and without blame or reproach—the broad question, "What have you done with your life?"

Fabienne, who "died" at age twelve, says she recalled all the events of her short life by feeling the joys and pains of the people with whom she had gone through these events. Betty talks about this life review when she encounters the being of light that she considers her Lord:

> I knew that he was aware of all my sins and faults, but that they didn't matter right now. He just wanted to hold me and share his love with me, and I wanted to share mine with him.[22]

In Moody's bestseller, *Life After Life*:

> When the light appeared, the first thing he said to me was, "What do you have to show me that you've done with your life?" or something to this effect. And that's when these flashbacks started…. It's not like he was trying to see what I had done—he knew already—but he was picking out these certain flashbacks of my life and putting them in front of me so that I would have to recall them. All through this, he kept stressing the importance of love…. He seemed very interested in things concerning knowledge, too…. He said that it is a continuous process, so I got the feeling that it goes on after death. I think that he was trying to teach me, as we went through those flashbacks.[23]

From Kenneth Ring's *Heading Toward Omega: In Search of the Meaning of the Near-Death Experience*:

> Instantly, my entire life was laid bare and open to this wonderful presence, "GOD." I felt inside my being his forgiveness for the things in my life I was ashamed of, as though they were not of great importance. I was asked—but there were no words; it was

a straight mental instantaneous communication—"What had I done to benefit or advance human race?" At the same time all my life was presently instantly in front of me and I was shown or made to understand what counted. I am not going into this any further, but, believe me, what I had counted in my life as unimportant was my salvation and what I thought was important was nil.[24]

You judge in the same way that everyone else does, but I don't judge anyone. If I did judge, I would judge fairly, because I would not be doing it alone. The Father who sent me is here with me (John 8:15–16).

7. A Sense of Peace and Tranquility

This sense is profound; it surpasses the current life experience with a reinforced sense of integrity and clarity.

Somehow an unexpected peace descended upon me. I found myself floating on the ceiling over the bed looking down at my unconscious body. I barely had time to realize the glorious strangeness of the situation—that I was me but not in my body—when I was joined by a radiant being bathed in a shimmering white glow. Like myself, this being flew but had no wings. I felt a reverent awe when I turned to him; this was no ordinary angel or spirit, but he had been sent to deliver me. Such love and gentleness emanated from his being that I felt that I was in the presence of the messiah.[25]

I give you peace, the kind of peace that only I can give. It isn't like the peace that this world can give. So don't be worried or afraid (John 14:27).

8. The Return

The return is either voluntary or involuntary, but always difficult. People hesitate to come back "to earth" since they are so comfortable wherever they have been. After this experience, which is often described as marvelous and luminous, the return to "the land of the living" happens reluctantly.

> I saw Christ, but the light coming from Him was so bright that in normal circumstances, I would have been blinded by it. I felt as if I wanted to stay here forever, but someone who seemed to be my guardian angel said, "You must go back where you came from; this is not yet your time." I then felt a kind of vibration and I was suddenly back where I came from.[26]

And Betty recounts her experience in "My Return," chapter 18 of her book:

> No good-byes were said; I simply found myself in the hospital room again. The door was still half open, the light was on above the sink, and lying on the bed under the blankets was my body.... I started jerking around inside [my body] as though many volts of electricity were pulsing through me. I felt the pain and sickness of my body again, and I became inconsolably depressed. After the joy of spiritual freedom, I had become prisoner to the flesh again.[27]

She explains very clearly the difficulty for experiencers to talk about their NDEs:

> For the next few hours, nurses and doctors were in and out, checking on me. Although they were paying much more attention to me than they had the night before, neither Joe nor I shared anything of my experience with them. The next morning one of the doctors said, "You really had a hard time last night. Can you tell me what you experienced?" I found that I couldn't share it with him, and I said I had nightmares. I was discovering that it was difficult for me to talk about my journey beyond, and it wasn't long before I didn't even want to share more of it with Joe. Talking seemed to dilute it. The experience was sacred. A few weeks passed and I did share more of it with Joe and the older children.

They immediately supported me, dispelling any fears I had of telling my family what had happened. I had a lot of learning and growing to do in the years ahead. In fact, the next few years would be the most difficult of my life.[28]

In chapter 19, "My Recovery," she explains:

I began sinking into a deep depression. I couldn't forget the scenes of beauty and peace of the spirit world, and I wanted terribly to return there. As the world whirled around me, I became fearful of life, even loathing it at times, praying for death. I asked God to take me home, to please, please release me from this life and unknown mission. I became agoraphobic, fearing to leave the house. I remember times when I would look out the window to the mailbox and wish that I had the courage to go to it. I was sinking into myself, dying a slow death, and although Joe and the children were wonderfully supportive, I knew that I was slipping away from them.

Finally it was love for my family that saved me.... It didn't happen all at once, but life became enjoyable again. Although my heart never truly left the spirit world, my love for this life flourished and became stronger than ever.[29]

Whether I live or die, I always want to be as brave as I am now and bring honor to Christ. If I live, it will be for Christ, and if I die, I will gain even more. I don't know what to choose. I could keep on living and doing something useful. It is a hard choice to make. I want to die and be with Christ, because that would be much better. But I know that all of you still need me (Philippians 1:20–24).

9. Repercussions on One's Way of Life

Surely, no one escapes from such an experience without consequences. One must readapt to normal life. A feeling of culpability—that sometimes requires psychotherapy—occasionally happens from having considered leaving loved ones behind. This feeling nonetheless indicates that death is not sought after.

Whatever the case, those who encounter the being of light are transformed and deeply marked: No matter a person's religion, beliefs, or philosophy, such an experience brings a new or renewed desire for spirituality. Subsequently, one has a different rapport with death; one puts love of the other ahead of all else, and assures whoever wants to listen that life does not end at the time of death and that the afterlife is magnificent.

The testimonies that Jeffrey Long gathered on the NDERF website suggest something of note: *In their own way, NDEs have a healing effect on almost everyone who experiences them.*

Still, life continues, and the experiencers do not necessarily become saints or spiritual masters. Similar to people I have known who are miraculously cured at Lourdes, there is a distinct before and after for them: they experience something so powerful that they cannot think of life in the same way.[30] They do not tend to brag; they remain modest and do not seek to put their story ahead of other people's experiences.

What remains constant is that those who return from an NDE are not afraid of death. They most definitely do not seek it either, since they dislike the idea of suicide. They might be afraid of the process of dying but not of death itself, because they know that death is the beginning of something incredible. They usually become less materialistic and stronger believers in God. In their relationships with others, they develop a great interest in values based on love. This makes a big difference in their lives.

> I don't fear death. Those feelings have vanished. I don't feel bad at funerals anymore. I kind of rejoice at them, because I know what the dead person has been through.[31]

It can take time to integrate the idea that one has experienced fusion or love. Having these experiences does not mean that neuroses will magically disappear. People's psyches remain human and fragile. Still, life in general benefits from more depth. Near-death experience survivors become more in tune with their conscience and their spirit, and they get more engaged in religious life.

> Before my experience, I guess I was like most people struggling with a better self-image. But I really *experienced* how precious and

how loved I am by God—the light—and I am constantly reminded of that in my daily life.[32]

Almost all testimonies emphasize a unique and profound love of neighbor.

> Now ... I find that everyone I meet, I like. I very rarely meet someone I don't like. And that's because I accept them right away as someone I like. I don't judge people. And people respond to me in the same way and I think that they can feel this in me....
>
> I often think, "If He values me so much (as I experienced it that January day), then no matter what bad thoughts I may think about myself—I *have* to be a worthwhile person."[33]

A general and indubitable conclusion: almost all experiencers stop calling themselves atheists following their experience! They can no longer refute an afterlife.

> For now there are faith, hope, and love. But of these three, the greatest is love (1 Corinthians 13:13).

Frightening Near-Death Experiences

To wrap up, it is important to understand that people also experience frightening NDEs, though it is difficult to know what percentage.[34] This is true because few of the people who experience them want to report these experiences, preferring instead to repress them. Also, it seems easier and more gratifying to ignore them rather than take them seriously, and to rely instead on more pleasant NDEs, which remain in the majority. (It seems many authors have helped make it so.)

The cardiologist Maurice Rawlings was the first to report on a resuscitated patient who said he had been to hell before returning to consciousness.[35] These cases are now considered unique, perhaps to help the people who experience them. As palliative care nurse Penny Sartori says, it is primordially necessary to support patients who undergo these experiences and to know where to refer for appropriate therapy; those who suffer after their return do not always know where to turn.[36] Currently, the Swiss Institute for Noetic Sciences (NOESIS Center) in Geneva offers psychotherapeutic support for people who have undergone such painful experiences.[37]

The various studies on the matter cannot seem to come up with reasons for these frightening experiences. Different hypotheses have been proposed to understand them, and all of them vary and seem to depend more on the observer rather than the experiencer. Of note is that these experiences do not only happen to "bad people." It is possible, but who are we to judge people's hearts? Can we objectively report on "good" versus "bad people"?

The various testimonies demonstrate that the afterlife is not all rosy and that it depends on the life we have lived on earth, including our religious experiences and our teachings. We will see one enlightening example of this in the fifth testimony, that is, Gloria Polo's experience: "I Came Close to Hell!"

Finally, are we not skimming over a spiritual origin?

There is good reason to call these experiences "frightening" rather than "negative," since in spite of their terrifying and traumatizing nature, they are like warnings from the other side: people return persuaded that they need to reorient their priorities so they do not go through the same experience after their death.

Your heart will always be where your treasure is (Matthew 6:21).

—⦵⦵⦵—

SECOND TESTIMONY

"NDE in Children"

In her last book, Dr. Elisabeth Kübler-Ross was primarily concerned with children suffering from terminal illnesses. "These children," she writes, "know what awaits them after life." Those who prepare for death—instead of being afraid of it and fighting against it—offer us lessons on life and its meaning.

Here is the story of a dying child's last moments, a testimony that is far from exceptional. A nurse was asking a seven-year-old child suffering from leukemia how he imagined paradise:

"It's like passing through a wall into another galaxy," he answered. "It's like walking through your brain, or in a cloud. The spirit is there but not the body."

"Do you know why people are so afraid of death?" asked the inquisitive nurse.

"If you're not attached to your body," replied the child, "if you allow things to happen, it's not really painful."

"Do you think that this life on earth is the only life we live?" the nurse insisted.

"Those who think so are mistaken," the child confirmed. "I know that I will come back someday."

Before death, children will often have out-of-body experiences and have encounters with other beings that await them on "the other side" to guide and help them. The church has called these beings "guardian angels." Most mystics and religious figures have called them "guides." I had encounters with them, and I called them "ferrymen." Others have called them "watchmen." It does not matter what we call them. It's essential to remember that each human being, from his first inhale to his last exhale, from his birth to the end of his physical existence, will be accompanied by one of these guides as he transitions to the other side, where there is neither physical body nor time and space.

On the threshold of death, children reach a certain sagacity that many adults envy, and this makes children sometimes react in unusual ways. Suzy, a young leukemia patient, realized as she saw her death approaching that she could increasingly leave her physical body. Her mother, who was watching her day and night, kept telling her, "Don't leave me, dear one. I won't be able to live without you." Suzy, who was slowly getting ready to die, became aware of life after death. One night, when she was in an altered state of consciousness, she had an out-of-body experience where she realized that she could travel without her physical shell; she was free to fly wherever she wanted. Her connection with a new, difficult-to-explain reality made her adopt an attitude often found among dying children. One evening, as Suzy felt her death approaching, she said to her mother, "Go home and rest a bit. You are very tired. You can come back tonight." The mother minded her daughter's wish, and Suzy took advantage of her mother's absence to pass through the gateway that separates earthly life from the other life. It was as if, in a moment of lucidity, she was able to distance herself from the person whose love and incomprehension could have hindered her transition.

Here's one of the most beautiful stories as told by Dr. Kübler-Ross. A four-year-old named Peter was declared dead after he had an allergic reaction to a certain medication. His desperate mother clung to her child, asking him to return. After what seemed like an eternity, Peter opened his eyes and said in the voice of a wise old man, "Mommy, I was dead. I was in a beautiful place, the most beautiful place one can imagine. I didn't want to come back. I saw Jesus and Mary. Mary said that it was not yet my time to leave this earth. I tried to ignore her, but Mary noticed. She then shoved me, saying, 'You must return to save your mother from the fire.'" It's at this moment that Peter opened his eyes. "You know, Mommy," he added, "when Mary said this, I ran toward the house again."

Peter's mother was a simple, pious woman. She didn't dare tell anyone about this for several years. Little by little, she was taken by depression because of her false interpretation of Mary's statement to her son. She believed that Peter needed to save her from hell. She didn't understand why she had been condemned to eternal damnation. She hadn't comprehended that it was meant to be symbolically interpreted.

First, if Peter saw Mary and Jesus, this could be due to the religious and cultural environment in his midst. They could just as well have been disincarnated beings, masters, or guides to whom he assigned names he knew. Furthermore, the fire that Peter's encountered being had mentioned was likely also a symbolic fire. Thirteen years after this incident, Peter's mother met with Dr. Kübler-Ross and told her the story. Dr. Kübler-Ross then told the woman to stop for a moment, to question her intuition—her deepest self. She then asked her, "What would have happened to you if Peter had not returned?" The mother held her head in her hands and cried out, "My God! It would have been hell!"[1]

A Lived Experience

I received this life story in Lourdes, February 11, 2014, on the occasion of the World Day of the Sick, established by John Paul II in 1992 during the Our Lady of Lourdes festivities. I was asked to offer it as is. It clearly does not consist of an NDE, but it is nonetheless a similar experience with an opening on heaven. It could be called a reverie, such as can commonly be found in the scriptures.

The Lord gave me two beautiful sons, one born in 1974 (and deceased in 1994) and the other in 1977. He wanted to give me another child. I was thirty-three years old at the time. But for various reasons (that I regret ...) I did not want to go through with this pregnancy. I therefore sought an abortion in December 1982. At the time, I didn't have a sense that it was really a child. My reasoning to go through the abortion was really strong, such that I could not conceive of the notion that I was carrying life within me. For me, this child did not exist; I could only feel a void in myself. And then the abortion was allowed, so... Some ten years later, while I was not thinking about this, the Lord, with his great generosity, showed me this child in a nocturnal vision. Imagine my surprise!

Here's how it happened. I had the feeling I was levitating, all the way up. I met up with a serene child (who somewhat resembled my second son) who told me he was mine and his name was Camille! He didn't seem like a ten-year-old child, the age he would have been on earth. At his side, another child asks him, "You don't blame her for what she did to you?" Camille answered, "No, I forgive her." At this point, I was dumbfounded! I had never asked for anything, and here I was learning that I had another child, that he was in "heaven," that his name was Camille, and that he had freely and generously forgiven me for having killed him! Thank you, Lord. What a great blessing! I want to therefore testify, today, that a child is a child starting at conception, that an abortion is a child's murder, that it brings great suffering for the mother (and perhaps for the child), and that we must absolutely take this into consideration. But the Lord, in his great goodness, does not leave any child behind who is happy in his Father's heart. A thousand thanks, dear Lord! The Lord is good!

Historical Comparisons

The NDE is one of the most important phenomena of human life. In examining it, we might gain a different perspective in understanding life after death from a rational perspective.
　—Raymond Moody

Brief History

The testimonies on the "signs of life" reported from the other side are universal and apply to all religious traditions. Near-death experiences are not twenty-first-century New Age novelties in need of some kind of revelation. It seems they have always existed and have primarily been recounted in the Christian literature through texts that correlate with modern-day NDEs.

Thus, in the sixth century, Gregory of Tours, a Frank historian, recounted the testimony of a certain Salvi who, after he was believed dead, came back to life shouting,

> Merciful Lord, what did you do to me to allow me to return in this dark place that serves as a dwelling place for the masses while your mercy in heaven was preferable to this detestable life on earth. Four days ago, while you saw me listless in the trembling cell, I was apprehended by two angels and taken to the heights of the heavens such that I imagined having under my feet not only the hideous world of this century but also the sky, the clouds, and the stars. Then, through an even brighter passageway than this ineffable light, an indescribable amplitude: it was shielded by a multitude of people of both sexes to such an extent that it was impossible to guess the breadth or depth of the crowd. And I heard a voice that said, "This man must return to the century

because he is necessary to our churches." Only the voice was audible; the speaker was impossible to discern. After having said those words much to the astonishment of those present, God's saint began to speak again with tears in his eyes, "Pity on me for I have dared to reveal such a mystery."[1]

In his book *La mort, et après ?* (Death, and then?), Michel Aupetit recalls several NDEs from the eighth century, written about by the monk and historian Saint Bede the Venerable, and from the twelfth century (supplied by Benedictine historian Guibert of Nogent) with comparable characteristics to modern-day NDEs: exit from the body, accompaniment by one or several angels, meetings with deceased relatives, delightful vision and perception, ineffable light, promise of delights, regret for having to return to earth.[2]

At the end of the Middle Ages, around 1500, Hieronymus Bosch painted the image titled *Ascent into the Empyrean or Highest Heaven*—a painting the corresponds so incredibly to people's NDE experiences that he was either inspired or he experienced an NDE himself.[3]

Through the centuries, many mystics had experiences similar to NDEs. The most well-known are: Catherine of Siena (1347–1380), Teresa of Avila (1515–1582), Anne Catherine Emmerich (1774–1824), and others.

The first known study of this phenomenon was conducted in 1892 by a reputable Swiss geologist and highlander, Professor Albert Heim, who had an NDE during a tumble where he almost lost his life. He collected and published the reports of some thirty climbers who had lived through similar accidents and had the same kind of experience.

When Raymond Moody started to talk about NDEs, he was a professor of philosophy and still a student in medicine.[4] He said that he was not raised in a religious household but that he was very soon interested in philosophy. In 1962, during his first year at the University of Virginia, he had read Plato's *The Republic* in which there is a story of a certain soldier named Er who was declared dead on the battlefield but who came back to life spontaneously. His book has made people talk. He has only been criticized in the United States by fundamentalist Christians.

His book was further popularized by Dr. Elisabeth Kübler-Ross's studies on death and dying. She was the first to approach this topic from a scientific perspective in the 1960s. *To appropriately broach the subject of humanity,* she surmised, *one must approach it from a holistic perspective: physical, emotional, intellectual, and spiritual.* She repeatedly said that her real task is to declare that "death does not exist." In 1977, Raymond Moody's book reached the other side of the Atlantic thanks to the famous composer Paul Misraki, who translated it.

In 1980, journalist Patrice Van Eersel went on a quest in the United States for the magazine *Actuel.* He was seeking to create a series titled *The Black Source.*[5] Ten years later, he wrote *Réapprivoiser la mort* (Getting reacquainted with death), where he demonstrates how the notion of NDE was originally suppressed in France, especially under the influence of ardent defenders of euthanasia, while in Anglo-Saxon countries, palliative care was being developed. His book popularized the French branch of the International Association for Near-Death Studies (IANDS-France). The latter was founded in 1987 by Evelyne-Sarah Mercier, who found herself in the midst of the New Age movement, a globalizing effort that presented itself as the epitome of humanity's spiritual evolution.[6]

In France, Dr. Jean-Pierre Jourdan, who was responsible for medical research at IANDS-France, published *Les Preuves scientifiques d'une vie après la vie* (Scientific proof of a life after life), and Dr. Jean-Jacques Charbonier, physician, anesthesiologist, and resuscitator in Toulouse, published *L'Après-vie existe* (The afterlife exists). The theme was the topic of the First International Medical Conference on Near-Death Experiences, a foundational conference held on June 17, 2006, in Martigues, which gathered over two thousand people. The conference was launched and organized by a remarkable young woman, Sonia Barkallah, who was passionately interested in this issue and who claimed that Dr. Moody's book saved her life at a time when she was tempted by suicide. Four years prior, she had produced a documentary film on the matter, *Un autre regard sur la mort* (Another look at death). Through the course of making the film, she discovered that numerous works and research were under way in all parts of the world and in extremely diverse scientific disciplines.[7]

Finally, in 2013, Dr. Jeffrey Long published his book *Life After Death,* which surveys over thirteen hundred testimonies from all over the world—from all faiths, all ages, and all sources. Since the Internet is so readily accessible now compared with several years ago, such a complex census was easily possible. This also coincides with the fact that, as I have said before, resuscitations are much more frequent nowadays, which leads to more NDEs.

It is important to understand that the data are based on individual testimonies, and we know that testimonies are delicate. Still, it is fascinating to note that we are talking about an experience that is universal and that transcends all ages and civilizations. Testimonies are similar no matter the subject's source, the time in which the person lived; no matter the person's age, social milieu, intellectual abilities, religion or lack of faith, and whether the person lived in the West or not. But the testimonies are never identical. Each person lives it in his own way and conveys it according to his words, culture, temperament, psychology, and memories. There is no "cut and paste." Whoever experienced an NDE holds a distinctly personal memory of the impressions this altered state has left on his psyche.

It should also not be surprising to note that the experiencers have a great sensibility toward spirituality; some have chosen to dedicate their lives to priesthood or other aspects of religious life following their experience. Certain specialists have tried to establish tests and measures to evaluate the "quality" of NDEs.[8] Their usefulness is questionable because they are culturally influenced and difficult to apply to the great variety of experiences. In fact, with a little experience and sensibility, it is relatively easy to distinguish serious people who relate the facts as they are from those who feign or embellish their experience. In any case, it is not recommended to systematically doubt each testimony as is unless one admits that he is no longer trusting of human beings altogether.[9] A genuine testimony touches one deeply, and this is true for both the person who offers it (life is no longer the same) and the person who receives it. I have witnessed many of these stories in Lourdes through people sharing their healings.

Some questions remain unchanged: Why do some people experience this "false start"? Why are they not meant to die? Why are they given a second chance? There is no universal answer.[10] The hour of death is not dependent on us, thankfully so. In any case, the person who returns knows why he returned. Here also, the answer is completely personal but corresponds with other people's answers.

And Nowadays?

Some scientists, who are courageous enough to confront the criticisms of their peers, are attempting to understand these unusual events whose existence has often been denied if not rejected by science. Their hope is to better understand the origins and mechanisms of consciousness. Armed with the tools of mental imagery, they explore the brain and experiment without presumptions. They are ready to admit that the phenomenon could be linked to a neuronal deregulation, or they may be willing to identify the existence of a sixth sense, as long as the methods are rigorous in nature. Canadian neuroscience researcher Mario Beauregard set up video monitors in a Montreal hospital's coronary unit in order to study the NDE phenomenon. Swiss neurologist Olaf Blanke is studying the phenomenon of disembodiment. Researcher Eric Dutoit, doctor of clinical psychology and psychopathology, is responsible for the *Unité de soins et de recherche sur l'esprit* (USRE) (Unit of Care and Research on the Spirit) at the Timone University Hospital in Marseille.

The Near Death Experience Research Foundation (NDERF) works with research teams in Switzerland, Canada, and the United States on the phenomena of NDE and disembodiment. Dr. Jeffrey Long, founder of NDERF, upholds that *near-death experiences are real. Witnesses of all ages, all nationalities, and all religions often recount that they have seen or heard things while unconscious and separated from their body; there is no physiological explanation to solve this mystery.*

These experiences are also a research topic in scientific parapsychology. The Parapsychological Association, representing a group of scientists and students who study telepathy and psychokinesis, is a member of the reputable American Association for the Advancement of Science (AAAS); a division of perceptual studies was created at the University of Virginia; a center for the study of abnormal psychological processes was created at the University of Northampton in England, which already accounts for eight university settings integrating parapsychological disciplines. Other research efforts are underway at the Center for Research on Consciousness and Anomalous Psychology at Lund University in Sweden and the Department of Psychology and Parapsychology at Andhra University in India.

For the last few years, the Catholic University in Lyon, France, offers its students an elective titled *Sciences, société et phénomènes dits paranormaux* (Science, society, and so-called paranormal phenomena). In France still, a center for the study of NDE directed by the professor of philosophy and psychologist Marc-Alain Descamps is gathering testimonies. Sonia Barkallah, who founded with Dr. Jean-Pierre Postel the *Centre national d'étude, de recherche et d'information sur la conscience* (CNERIC) (National Center for Consciousness Study, Research, and Information), continues her work on the topic.

Contrary to what is expected, science is serious about the study of NDEs and similar phenomena, despite what Sonia Barkallah says about *many physicians and researchers who continue to choose to not get involved for fear that they'll be considered at least eccentric if not charlatans.*

I have already spoken about the NOESIS Center in Geneva, also known as the Swiss Institute for Noetic Sciences, founded in 1999 by research director Sylvie Dethiollaz and psychotherapist Claude Charles Fourrier.

Finally, I wish to highlight the Second International Medical Conference on Near-Death Experiences organized by Ms. Barkallah in March 2013 in Marseille, where Dr. Moody was again present and where new information about NDEs was presented.[11] Here is a summary of the conference proceedings by Jocelin Morisson:

In 2006, the first meetings in Martigues laid the groundwork for developing a summation of thirty years of research and reflection on NDEs. These second meetings demonstrated how research on NDEs is flourishing in spite of the inherent challenges. They have also shown how our reflections on the matter are enriched with each new revelation, which is somewhat connected with the high state of emergency of our societies, indeed with the projected "end of a world" in 2012. Yes, we must find radical alternatives to the status quo, and the study of NDEs invites us and compels us to seek a new understanding of Man. This in turn can lead us to reinvent—if not simply invent—to commune more with others by disrupting our rapport with death and therefore with life. In fact, near-death experiences are not the only experiences implicated in the approach of death. Researchers and clinicians are now considering a number of perimortem phenomena (that is, phenomena surrounding death) that include so-called empathic or shared NDEs—experienced by the loved ones and companions of the dying[12]—but also phenomena like "greater consciousness as death approaches," "visions of the dying," "terminal lucidity," as well as experiences of "contact with the deceased" soon after death. It's hard not to recognize the relative proximity of these experiences and the amazing consistency between them. Such consistency, and the difficulty in accounting for it within the realm of a materialistic and reductionist science, leads even the most rigorous of researchers such as Raymond Moody to "give way," that is, to abandon the original skepticism that would keep one from arriving at conclusions, which was his position for fifty years. He currently admits to being convinced of the persistence of some form of existence after death.[13]

The bodies we now have are weak and can die. But they will be changed into bodies that are eternal. Then the scriptures will come true: "Death has lost the battle! Where is its victory? Where is its sting?" (1 Corinthians 15:54–55).

—◦◊◦—

THIRD TESTIMONY

"Paradise Exists"

Dr. Eben Alexander, an American neurosurgeon and brain specialist as well as a skeptic and Cartesian, was a resolute nonbeliever about the existence of any life after death. He believed all accounts of near-death experiences were the result of delirium and foolishness. This lasted until November 2008, when a devastating meningitis shattered his convictions. He revealed, both in the headlines of *Newsweek* magazine and in his book, *Proof of Heaven: A Neurosurgeon's Journey into the Afterlife*, that he had had a near-death experience—a journey that convinced him of the existence of life after death.[1]

I grew up in a scientific world, the son of a neurosurgeon. I followed my father's path and became an academic neurosurgeon, teaching at Harvard Medical School and other universities. I understand what happens to the brain when people are near death, and I had always believed there were good scientific explanations for the heavenly out-of-body journeys described by those who narrowly escaped death. The brain is an astonishingly sophisticated but extremely delicate mechanism. Reduce the amount of oxygen it receives by the smallest amount and it will react. It was no big surprise that people who had undergone severe trauma would return from their experiences with strange stories.... However, after seven days in a coma during which the human part of my brain, the neocortex, was inactivated, I experienced something so profound that it gave me a scientific reason to believe in consciousness after death. I know how pronouncements like mine sound to skeptics, so I will tell my story with the logic and language of the scientist I am. Very early one morning four years ago, I awoke with an extremely intense headache. Within hours, my entire cortex—the part of the brain that controls thought and emotion and that in essence makes us human—had shut down. Doctors at Lynchburg General Hospital in Virginia, a hospital where I myself worked as a neurosurgeon, determined that I had somehow contracted a very rare bacterial meningitis that mostly attacks newborns. E. coli bacteria had penetrated my cerebrospinal fluid and were eating my brain. When I entered the emergency room that morning, my chances of survival in anything beyond a vegetative state were already low. They soon sank to near nonexistent…. While the neurons of my cortex were stunned to complete inactivity by the bacteria that had attacked them, my brain-free consciousness journeyed to another, larger dimension of the universe: a dimension I'd never dreamed existed and which the old, pre-coma me would have been more than happy to explain was a simple impossibility. Toward the beginning of my adventure, I was in a place of clouds. Big, puffy, pink-white ones that showed up sharply against the deep blue-black sky. Higher than the clouds—immeasurably higher—flocks of transparent, shimmering beings arced across the sky, leaving long, streamer-like lines behind them. Birds? Angels? These words registered later, when I was writing down my recollections. But neither of these words do justice to the beings themselves, which were quite simply different from anything I have known on this planet. They were more advanced. Higher forms.[2]

Dr. Alexander recalls having heard "a sound, huge and booming like a glorious chant, [coming] down from above," which provided him with much joy. Later in his journey, he was accompanied by a woman. "She was young, and I remember what she looked like in complete detail. She had high cheekbones and deep-blue eyes. Golden brown tresses framed her lovely face," he explains, adding that they were both traveling on the wings of a butterfly. "In fact, millions of butterflies were all around us—vast fluttering waves of them, dipping down into the woods and coming back up around us again. It was a river of life and color, moving through the air.[3]

Was this due to delirium? Or a cerebral malfunction? Or too much morphine? The neurosurgeon, who until then had never believed in NDEs, pledged that everything was indeed real and that it was not "some passing and insubstantial fantasy."

> As far as I know, no one before me has ever traveled to this dimension (a) while their cortex was completely shut down, and (b) while their body was under minute medical observation, as mine was for the full seven days of my coma. All the chief arguments against near-death experiences suggest that these experiences are the results of minimal, transient, or partial malfunctioning of the cortex. My near-death experience, however, took place not while my cortex was malfunctioning, but while it was simply off. This is clear from the severity and duration of my meningitis, and from the global cortical involvement documented by CT scans and neurological examinations. According to current medical understanding of the brain and mind, there is absolutely no way that I could have experienced even a dim and limited consciousness during my time in the coma, much less the hyper-vivid and completely coherent odyssey I underwent.... Seeing and hearing were not separate in this place where I now was. Everything was distinct, yet everything was also a part of everything else, like the rich and intermingled designs on a Persian carpet.... I know full well how extraordinary, how frankly unbelievable, all this sounds. Had someone—even a doctor—told me a story like this in the old days, I would have been quite certain that they were under the spell of some delusion. But what happened to me was, far from being delusional, as real or more real than any event in my life. That includes my wedding day and the birth of my two sons.[4]

Since this near-death experience, Dr. Alexander no longer has any doubts that consciousness is neither produced in nor limited by the brain, much as leading scientific thought would like to believe. It extends well beyond the body.

> The plain fact is that the materialist picture of the body and brain as the producers, rather than the vehicles, of human consciousness

is doomed. In its place a new view of mind and body will emerge, and in fact is emerging already. This view is scientific and spiritual in equal measure and will value what the greatest scientists of history themselves always valued above all: truth.[5]

It took months for Dr. Alexander to accept what happened to him and to speak freely and openly about it. He now intends "to spend the rest of my life investigating the true nature of consciousness and making the fact that we are more, much more, than our physical brains as clear as I can, both to my fellow scientists and to people at large."[6]

———

A Bet

God is, or he isn't.

The conundrum imposes itself; we must indeed choose because, anyway we look at it, we are "implicated" in existence. Maybe God does not exist and I live my life without him. At the time of death, I risk discovering everything that I have missed!

Maybe God, who is Love, exists, and I decide to live my whole life on earth with Him. At the time of death, I discover Truth!

If I lose, I lose nothing!

If I win, I win everything!

—Blaise Pascal
  Pensées (Thoughts)
  Brunschvicg Edition #23

———

A Scientific Problem

One thing is certain: To this day, there is no rational explanation for the phenomenon of NDE. All scientists who have attempted to figure out the workings of this experience have failed miserably.
   —Dr. Jean-Jacques Charbonier

When I speak to colleagues about near-death experiences, most of them immediately respond, "NDEs? It is most certainly a natural phenomenon. There will someday be a rational justification for them." They categorically reject these experiences as too personal, believing that what might happen after death cannot be the object of experimental studies. Yet in acknowledging the multiple facts at our disposal and the coherence of people's stories, we cannot graciously eliminate the problem or allow ourselves to brush aside the facts at hand.

We must set aside the opinions of those who make a living at systematically denigrating anything that more or less involves spirituality—and, let us admit it, NDEs are included in this. Such denigration is the case with the Skeptics Society in the United States, the *Zététique* in France, and with certain authors such as Michel Onfray or Philippe Wallon.

Knowing that these phenomena are not easily integrated within the traditional scientific opus, true scientists ask these two fundamental questions: Do NDEs really exist? How do we explain them?

Prior to answering, let us make an important distinction: from a medical perspective, there is a difference between clinical death and biological death.

Clinical death is distinguished by subjective signs: nonreactive bilateral pupillary dilation, cardiac arrest, and flat electroencephalogram (EEG). In the subsequent fifteen to twenty seconds that follow cardiac arrest, there is indeed a cessation of cerebral activity that can be verified through a flat EEG: the cortex is no longer functioning and there is no possible sensorial activity. This *cerebral death* is currently considered a *state of clinical death*.

After twenty minutes, cerebral lesions are extremely serious and irreversible. Resuscitation is generally only possible in the first three to ten minutes. Accordingly, a donor organ must be taken soon after blood circulation stops but when a person "presents with a persistent cardiac and respiratory arrest"—that is, they are artificially maintained alive using resuscitation equipment—and this person has been diagnosed with *encephalitic death*.[1] It seems problematic, at the very least: a living organ must be taken from a dead body (whose respiration is artificially maintained to keep the organs intact[2]) while the brain is no longer functioning![3]

In turn, *biological death* is definitive, irreversible; it is a condition that manifests in the start of decomposition.

The Scientific Reality of Near-Death Experiences

It is important to clarify that NDEs do not happen after definitive death; they happen *at the edge of death* when life has not completely disappeared and when cells can still survive.

NDEs happen before irreversible biological death. That is indeed why the term "near death" is most appropriate.

Still, NDEs happen after "clinical death," that is, after cardiac arrest for sure, but also *after the end of cerebral cortex activity*. This might seem doubtful, but certain distinct experiences prove otherwise.

Thus, Dutch cardiologist Dr. Pim van Lommel published a scientific study on the topic in the prestigious publication *The Lancet* on December 15, 2001. The study was conducted on 344 patients successfully resuscitated from a coma secondary to cardiovascular arrest and considered clinically dead, that is, in a state of unconsciousness provoked by a lack of blood flow to the brain (cerebral death). Testimonies were gathered soon—within a week, at most—after the event (a necessary precaution to avoid embellishment or phantasm). Only 18 percent of interviewees described a "classic" NDE that included an exit from the body. This means that cerebral anoxia instigated by insufficient blood flow to the brain does not cause an NDE.[4]

Another study was completed by Dr. Sam Parnia, cardiologist at Southampton General Hospital in the United Kingdom, specialist in internal and respiratory medicine and intensive care, and researcher at Weill Cornell Medical Center in New York City.[5] He referenced sixty-nine people who were victims of heart attack and who were declared dead and then resuscitated; they were not given any oxygen or other substances liable to cause hallucinations. He noted that when a person is declared dead, that is, when the brain does not produce any activity (flat EEG), 10 to 20 percent of patients could experience an NDE.

It clearly seems that even when the brain ceases to function, *consciousness can continue.* The findings suggest that during the first few minutes after death, consciousness is not annihilated. We do not know if it recedes later, but immediately after death, consciousness is not lost, Parnia explains in the *Daily Mail.*[6]

Nonetheless, he continues, "We know that the brain cannot function when the heart stops beating." The results of his study are therefore important, considering that, until now, doctors assumed that people's stories of life after death were really hallucinations that occurred either before the heart stopped beating or after it was reanimated, Dr. Parnia says. These experiences were not assumed to correspond to events that occurred while the heart of the patient had stopped. Additionally, the scientist declares that his research subjects' memories of what occurred were consistent with actual facts.[7]

These well-conducted studies end up eliminating the counterhypotheses—whether physiological, psychological, pharmacological, or neurochemical—that attempt to denigrate NDEs: we can no longer hypothesize that it was caused by a cerebral anoxia, a hallucination, or a neuronal or hormonal disorder.

An NDE can occur during a functional transient loss of all of the functions of the cortex and nervous system. Near-death experiences can happen without any medication. There is no explanation for the first phase in which a dying person experiences peace and serenity; encounters with beings that were once strangers; the ability to see scenery from a perspective outside of the body; the detailed memories; the ability to see objects in an adjacent room; the descriptions of the caregivers' gestures, words, or thoughts; the transformation that follows the experience, etc.

What this means is that people who experience NDEs have "a thought process and a form of consciousness" independent of cerebral functions. Their perceptions seem to have increased tenfold and their consciousness is sharper.

We are dealing with a process that defies all physiological explanations.

A Scientific Challenge

These experiences make us question the nature of consciousness: We know that it is where thoughts, feelings, and memories reside. But where does consciousness itself reside? How is it connected to the external body? What is consciousness, really?

The state of consciousness that outlasts clinical death poses a major scientific challenge, since prevailing medical theory advances that it is the brain—and only the brain—that produces thoughts, which is something that is yet to be demonstrated. Nothing of the sort has ever been scientifically proven. For decades, many important studies have been conducted to locate consciousness and memory within the brain, but without success. At this time, science has little clue as to how brain cells can produce thoughts.

Those who defend the prevailing medical theory are against the notion of NDE; they believe there must be another origin to the reported events if NDEs occur when brain functions are dead. However, as Dr. Parnia demonstrates in his study—and Dr. van Lommel clearly shows in his writings—consciousness can function independently of brain activity. Similarly, the work of Dr. Melvin Morse, American pediatrician and specialist in children's NDEs, concludes that the right temporal lobe connects people's memories to a universal data bank that acts as a receptor-transmitter.[8]

This brings about the notion that the brain does not produce thoughts but instead acts as a transmitter of thoughts; it can be seen as a filter for consciousness. The theory that NDEs can only be explained by a separation of consciousness from the body has led NDE defenders to conclude that consciousness is separate from the brain, which revolutionizes the concepts that the scientific community has adopted up until now.[9]

One natural conclusion is that the brain is nothing but a receptor-transmitter, much like a radio station: when a radio station is compromised, it can no longer transmit the music, even when the orchestra is still playing.

Dr. van Lommel asks a series of questions that promote reflection: Can brain death really be translated as a simple "death" or is it instead the beginning of the process of death that can last many hours or even days? What happens to consciousness during this time? Should we not also consider the likelihood that a person, who is pronounced clinically dead after cardiac arrest, might remain conscious? Or the likelihood that some kind of consciousness could survive past the death of this person, when his body has turned cold? How is consciousness related to the integrity of brain function? Is it possible to understand the nature of this connection?[10]

These questions are interesting on more than one level; they are unacceptable to the materialist but they provide fodder for scientists who are open to the transcendent.

In any case, if there is validity to the conclusion that consciousness indeed persists beyond clinical death and that it can be experienced independent of brain activity, this could lead to a profound transformation in the Western medical paradigm. It could have implications toward ethical and practical issues in medicine, such as the treatment of comatose or dying patients, euthanasia, abortions, organ transplants, etc. It could lead to great ethical progress.

Moreover, the hypothesis of *consciousness* independent of the body seems to corroborate with what religions have claimed for millennia. We will investigate the details of this hypothesis within the Christian tradition.

> But when these tents are destroyed, we know that God will give each of us a place to live. These homes will not be buildings that someone has made, but they are in heaven and will last forever (2 Corinthians 5:1).

—◦◦◦—

"Life on Borrowed Time"

In order to understand the following story, it is necessary to go a long way back, to the Middle East, twelve hundred years before Jesus Christ: a nation—the sons of Israel and descendants of Abraham—settles in the Land of Canaan. This nation promotes faith in a single God, one that saved it from slavery in the Land of Egypt and led it to this Promised Land. United in God by his words, thanks to the ongoing succession of prophets, its long history will leave its mark on all of humanity.

Between 4 and 7 BCE, a child named Jesus is born in Bethlehem of Judea; he is the son of Mary, wife of Joseph, the carpenter from Nazareth. At thirty, Jesus travels across Palestine with his disciples and twelve apostles that he chose to be with him. He presents himself as the Son of God, who has come to the world to invite people to true life. He pronounces the good news of salvation as he heals the sick and forgives people's sins:

> If you are tired from carrying heavy burdens, come to me and I will give you rest. Take the yoke I give you. Put it on your shoulders and learn from me. I am gentle and humble, and you will find rest (Matthew 11:28–29).

At the same time, conditions for this new life that he proposes are very strict:

> If any of you want to be my followers, you must forget about yourself. You must take up your cross and follow me. If you want to save your life, you will destroy it. But if you give up your life

for me, you will find it. What will you gain, if you own the whole world but destroy yourself? What would you give to get back your soul?

The Son of Man will soon come in the glory of his Father and with his angels to reward all people for what they have done. I promise you that some of those standing here will not die before they see the Son of Man coming with his kingdom (Matthew 16:24–27).

Near the year 30 CE, on the eve of giving up his life and being nailed to the cross in Jerusalem, Jesus gathers his apostles to celebrate the Easter meal with them. During this meal, Jesus offers his body and his blood for humanity's redemption and access to eternal life. The next day, he dies crucified with two thieves at his sides. Three days later and in the weeks that follow, he presents himself to his disciples, raised from the dead, resurrected. They will bear witness to it until their martyr. As for Jesus, he will no longer die. Alive, he "rises to heaven," disappearing in front of their eyes after promising them the Spirit of God, the Holy Spirit, that they will receive on the day of the Pentecost.

Now that we have recalled this, here is Natalie Saracco's testimony, which I invite you to watch if you can on YouTube (www.youtube.com). Prior to this, one must read the Gospel according to John 19:31–34:

> The next day would be both a Sabbath and the Passover. It was a special day for the Jewish people, and they did not want the bodies to stay on the crosses during that day. So they asked Pilate to break the men's legs and take their bodies down. The soldiers first broke the legs of the other two men who were nailed there. But when they came to Jesus, they saw that he was already dead, and they did not break his legs.
>
> *One of the soldiers stuck his spear into Jesus's side*, and blood and water came out.

In 2008, Natalie had a terrible car accident on the freeway at 130 km/hr (80 mph). Trapped in a car, she exhibited all the signs of an internal hemorrhage, choking and spitting blood. Little by little, she felt life disappear from her body. Then, she said, in an out of "space-time location,

I found myself up close with Jesus, who was dressed in a white tunic."[1] She was experiencing a spectacular near-death experience. Suddenly, she found herself in front of Christ, who was showing her his pierced heart wrapped in a crown of thorns.

> He was crying and from his heart poured tears of blood. And his tears were pouring from my own heart, too. It's as if he wanted me to feel his severe suffering. It was such a concentrate of suffering that I lost my fear of dying, and those I was leaving. And I asked him, "Lord, why are you crying?" "I'm crying because you are my dear children and I gave my life for you, and in return, I see only coldness, contempt, and indifference. My heart is consumed by a fierce love for you, whoever you may be."[2]

Natalie Saracco elaborates that she knew God's love for all, but she could not have imagined such a burning love that it surpasses anything that can be conceived. Then, in an impulse, she tells Jesus:

> Lord, what a pity to render my soul now that I know you madly love us! I would love to be able to return to earth to bear witness of your mad love for us and to console your Sacred Heart![3]

She continues:

> At the moment that I pronounced those words, I found myself to be a little fragile being in front of a thick cloud: it was my hour of judgment as I stood in front of the heavenly tribunal. I then heard a voice say, "You will be judged according to the true love of God and of the brothers." As soon as I heard these words, it was like I was reinserted in my body: A warm sensation traversed my whole being from head to toe. I spontaneously stopped spitting blood. The firefighters pulled me out of the car. At the hospital, the doctors could not understand how I could have survived after such a crash. It was hard to explain. Furthermore, I was bathing in an extraordinary sense of peace and joy. I went from someone who was burned alive to feeling as if everything had reorganized and gathered itself in me.[4]

Here is a stunning NDE with, in addition, a testimony that astonishingly resembles the visions of Saint Margaret Mary of the sanctuary of Paray-le-Monial in 1675.[5] Through the course of many apparitions, in a moment of ecstasy, Christ came to Saint Margaret Mary and expressed his love by showing her his pierced heart, saying,

> Behold this Heart which has loved everyone so much that it has spared nothing, even to exhausting and consuming itself, in order to testify its love.... In recognition of this, all I receive from most in return are indignities.

Christ's transpierced heart—the Sacred Heart—was the paradoxical sign of the victory of love over death. This sign was an appeal for us to join our hearts with Christ's heart to receive love fully and completely and to find the way to true life.[6]

Two Thoughts

It's a strange weakness of the human spirit, for which death is never a presence, though it reveals itself in all places and in thousands of different forms. During funerals, people express astonishment over what the mortal has died of. Each person recollects in his own words the last time he spoke to the deceased and what the latter last uttered; and suddenly, he's dead. Here, they say, is what man is! And the one who says it is also a man; and that man does not apply it to himself, forgetful of his destiny! Or if some flight of fancy about preparing himself for death passes through him, he diminishes these dark ideas. And can I say, dear Sirs, that mortals do not care less for burying their thoughts about death than for burying the dead.

—Jacques-Bénigne Bossuet

What will happen on the other side when, for me, all will tumble into eternity ... I do not know! I believe, I only believe that a great love is waiting for me. But I do know that then I, poor and shabby, will let God carry the weight of my life. Do not think, however, that I will do this out of despair. No, I believe—I firmly believe—that a great love is waiting for me. Now that my hour is near, and the voice of eternity invites me to pass through the gate I will believe, still more, while stepping into death, what I have always believed. While walking, I will move into love. I will stretch out my arms toward his love ... moving gently down into life. When I die, do not cry, love will hold me peacefully. When I am afraid ... and why not? Remind me constantly, simply, that a great love is waiting for me. My Redeemer will open the gate of joy for me to his light. Yes, Father, look! I come to you. Like a child I throw myself into your love, your love that is waiting ... for me.

—Saint John of the Cross

Religious Approach

Our life is but a transitory journey,
A crossing over an ocean of impetuous enigmas:
True life awaits us on the shore!
  —Christian Charrière

From a religious perspective, it is difficult to be indifferent to near-death experiences. The meaning of life, existential questions, and confrontation with death are uncertainties that lead us to a metaphysical or religious investigation toward finding the answers.

Christianity affirms that Christ is the Son of God who lived an earthly life in Palestine two thousand years ago. It also affirms that he suffered for our sins, he offered his life for our benefit, he resurrected and returned from the dead to be forever living. He is our Savior: through his death, he conquered death, and death was put to death. Thanks to him, eternal life is offered to us; we can each find ourselves in God's presence and resurrected in his body. A Christian can absolutely leave it at that; the credo summarizes his whole faith.

Near-death experiences come as an additional offering.

We could easily do without them, much as we can do without actual miracles in lieu of our faith. No one is obligated to believe in them. They are signs that are freely given to us, and signs are free for the taking. Yet if they exist, why ignore them or even negate them? Of course, caution is still advised, as it is for other surprising facts such as apparitions and mystical phenomena. Certainly miracles are a fundamental part of the Catholic Church's corpus. This is never the case with NDEs, which are considered extraordinary events that threaten to induce the marvelous, risking even that we fall into illuminism or fideism.[1] Also, we should not be surprised that clerics interpret NDEs in a great variety of ways.

Swiss theologian Hans Küng believes that NDEs exist: We should not deny them; instead, we should interpret them.

Bishop Jean Vernette, who once was a delegate of the French episcopate responsible for inquiries related to sects and new religious phenomena, was faithfully allegiant to the discernment between NDEs and the Christian faith, eternal life and altered state of consciousness, resurrection and reincarnation, spiritual theology and parapsychology. His reasons for doing this were totally justified. Yet, as far as I know, he does not make a clear statement about NDEs.[2]

The person who has written the most on this topic is a fairly independent, atypical, and nonconformist theologian who has been freely critical of the church as institution—Father François Brune.[3] He presents a passionate thesis, though it is unfortunate that he blends the theme of NDE with that of a totally different concept: instrumental transcommunication (ITC), which attempts to communicate with the dead through technology. It is unfortunate because, as we know, attempting to communicate with the deceased can lead to connections with dangerous demonic entities. In fact, Father Brune himself admits that research on all that is paranormal or parapsychological can lead to a virtual catastrophe. This is especially the case in people whose psychological equilibrium is fragile, since they can be particularly attracted to such phenomena. He recognizes also that communication with the afterlife—including a seemingly benign phenomenon such as automatic writing—can lead to "possession."

That said, Father Brune offers several interesting reflections on NDEs as derived from a number of typical examples. He admits that at the time of death, when we will be as if *breathed in by God, but we will certainly need a time of purification—necessary for the simple reason that we could not yet stand it.* He thereby follows the doctrine of purgatory: *In order to live closely with God, one must first learn how to love like him,* he declares, *and spiritual growth continues in the afterlife.*[4] He then continues to tell us: *A great truth that is the outcome of all these testimonies of the afterlife is the complete respect for our liberty. As a consequence of this, our evolution and the rate of our evolution from one step to another, from one world to another, will depend on the good will of each of us.* For him, *it is at the time of death that we actualize our definite state of being without needing to wait for the end of times to retrieve a body. At the conclusion of this terrestrial life and thanks to the transformational power of the spirit, the soul is restored in a glorious, luminous body that carries within it an imprint of the physical body, which has been left on earth to disappear.*[5] Conversely, many religious people cannot admit the existence of this extravagant phenomenon, either because of their culture or their education. At best, they simply insist on the fact that these experiences are not elemental to faith and that all is revealed in the Revelation.

Of course, there is always a way to find contentment in the words of Moses, the prophets, what Jesus and the apostles have given us in the scriptures, and the whole Christian tradition. It would be easy to stick with what we know about death, the resurrection from death, and eternal life as they are elaborated upon in the credo. Still, why would God not give us a sign today much like the Shroud of Turin, which calls the attention of the modern person? What would be so unusual about that? What do we have to lose? It is not about proving anything: faith does not rely on proof. I nonetheless believe that there are some interesting "thought-provoking clues"[6] that clearly and gracefully bring reason and faith together.

Further, as we will see, the church can attest—after a complete authentication on all levels, of course—to the existence of apparitions, miracles, and even extraordinary phenomena that are difficult to explain and that are common in the experiences of saints and mystics: ecstasies, raptures, bilocation, etc., all of which defy understanding.

Then, we have the point of view of clerics who stand by the existence of NDEs. For instance, there is Bishop Michel Aupetit, physician and priest, who was once auxiliary bishop of the Paris diocese and is now bishop of Nanterre.[7] His reedited book, *La mort, et après?* (Death, and then?), is a must-read.

> For religions in general and for Catholicism specifically, it is appropriate to first investigate the neurophysiological reasons for these so-called extraordinary manifestations. If scientific research can give NDEs a logical explanation, it should be received with open arms. It's important to discern near-death experiences—that occur in patients in a state of clinical death whose flat electroencephalogram indicates a lack of brain activity—from extraordinary experiences—that happen to patients under the influence of a drug or a hallucinatory phenomenon of undetermined origins.

Currently, no psychological, pharmacological, or neurophysiological explanation has been offered to understand these experiences on the verge of death. When comparing them with our own Christian beliefs, there is nothing in them that is contradictory with our faith in eternal life.

Whatever the case, it's impossible to ignore all these subjective experiences, especially when we see that they are universally applicable and they overlap in fascinating ways. It's essential to first show our interest in these phenomena by respecting those who have experienced them and who often feel ostracized by the sarcasm of nonbelievers. We must look for natural causes, if there are any, and not let ourselves be led toward superficial or lofty reactions. In any event, believers can fully engage in a fruitful exploration of their hope and their faith. They then can draw forth the implications of such exploration, like most experimenters do, in order to live a better, more harmonious life with God and with others.[8]

His whole proposal is something to behold. Bishop Aupetit then takes up the fundamental question of the moment when "existential" life disappears, *the hour of death.*

Medicine has always had issue with this moment: it is one of the most difficult clinical diagnostics to declare, like that of the beginning of pregnancy (the two extremities of life). As was elaborated in the previous chapter, one must discern between "clinical" death and "biological" death; also, NDEs occur between clinical death and biological death.

Theologians further believe in what they call *metaphysical death* or *ontological death.* They are thereby demarking the moment of actual and definite separation of the soul from the body. It is the last frontier! It does not necessarily correspond to biological death. There is in fact a possible time lapse—of significant proportion—between physical death, biological death, and the possible "distancing" of the soul, according to those who accompany the dying and the Catholic tradition.[9] That lapse can average about three hours (and can last at least a half hour up to seven hours, as per the revelations of Marthe Robin, twentieth-century mystic). The person is physically dead but, somehow, stays around until a certain moment that can be witnessed by those around him, a moment where the soul definitely goes through to the other side. This constitutes metaphysical death.

Bishop Aupetit then states, rightfully so, that, *The limit reached by those who experience NDEs before returning "to their bodies" is possibly the real limit between life and death and the ultimate passageway where those who are registered in the Book of Life will be similar to God, because they will see him as he is* (Apostles 20:11–13, 1 John 3:2).

An NDE can occur just before this moment; it will eventually become a disembodiment. It is therefore a *reanimation* and not a *resurrection*. We will explore this again in the following chapters. Let this be an occasion to recall just how important this moment of death is: *a truly unique time of existence.* The church invites us to look after the suffering and to pray again at the side of those who recently passed. The period that surrounds death seems to be a time of battle between the forces of good and evil in the soul of the deceased; rather than ending with clinical death (and even biological death), this battle surely lasts until the moment when death is definite, that is, when the soul exits the body.

> I am the one who raises the dead to life! Everyone who has faith in me will live, even if they die. And everyone who lives because of faith in me will never really die. Do you believe this? (John 11:25–26).

As we enter into the following testimony by Gloria Polo, it is essential to know that the Catholic Church espouses three "states" in the other world: Each man receives in his immortal soul his eternal retribution at the moment of death; it comes in the form of a specific judgment that compares his life to Christ. Thus, he will either be directed to a purification (purgatory, which allows one to answer to God), or to his entrance in the heavenly beatitude (the saints whose terrestrial lives have clearly expressed the love they received from God), or to be immediately damned for an eternity (hell, a place of complete desolation for those who freely and knowingly reject God).

We are all made for God; we are created so as to enter into a completely pure connection with him. God gives each soul enough gifts that it can go directly to heaven. During our time on earth, we are offered all the opportunities to present ourselves as pure beings in front of God after our death. The trials that we suffer stand in place of a purgatory. Still, as is well known, we too often forget that we have an immortal soul, and we occupy ourselves instead with many other things. Thus, our purification is retarded. In his extreme mercy, the Lord accords us additional time, a delay of sorts, a new occasion to purify ourselves, a kind of additional step before heaven —what we call purgatory.

—◈—

FIFTH TESTIMONY

"I Came Close to Hell!"

Here then is the complete testimony by Dr. Gloria Polo, dental surgeon in Bogota, Columbia, a person no better or worse than any other. Nonetheless, she recounts her story of having brushed with hell during the course of a near-death experience and consequently having her perspective on life transformed![1] Can this testimony be taken literally? Like all testimonies, this one could have been embellished or tainted over time. It remains a good example that deserves to be read in its entirety.

It should be noted that a number of saints have reported on the visions of hell that they experienced, each equally shocking as the other.[2] For example, Saint Teresa of Avila wrote: "The Lord wanted to show me the place that the demons had prepared for me (in hell) and that I had merited for my sins." She speaks of this place so disgusting that even the slightest hope of consolation is forever banished.[3]

> Brothers and sisters, it's a miracle that I am here with you sharing this beautiful gift that I received from our Lord, ten years ago.
>
> This occurred in May of 1995 at the National University in Bogota. With my nephew, a dentist just like me, we were working on our master's thesis. My husband was with us that Friday afternoon since we needed to pick up some books at the university's dental school. It was raining heavily and my nephew and I went under a small umbrella. My husband, who was wearing a trench coat, was approaching the campus library. My nephew and I were following him but we headed toward some trees to avoid large puddles. At that moment, we were both struck by lightning. My nephew died on the spot. He was young but, in

spite of his age, his life was given to our Lord. He had been very devoted to the Baby Jesus; he carried his image in a crystal on his chest. According to the autopsy, the lightning entered through the image, charred his heart, and exited through his feet. His exterior was left intact; there were no traces of burns. The lightning burned my body horribly, both inside and outside. This body you now see was reconstructed through the grace of divine mercy. The lightning had completely burned me. My breasts were charred and almost all my flesh and a part of my ribs were gone. The lightning had exited through my right foot after having burned my stomach, liver, kidneys, and lungs.

I used an intrauterine device (IUD) made of copper as a form of birth control. Copper is an excellent electrical conductor, so it charred my ovaries. I was in cardiac arrest, lifeless, my body kept jerking from the electrical currents still affecting it. But this concerns only the physical side of me. While my flesh was burned, I found myself in a beautiful tunnel of white light, filled with joy and peace. No words can describe the gloriousness of this joyful moment. The apotheosis of this instant was immense.

I felt happy and full of joy, since I was no longer subjected to the law of gravity. At the end of the tunnel, I saw something like a sun shining extraordinarily bright. I will describe it as white to give you a sense of it but, in fact, there is no color on earth that can compare to the brightness and intensity of this light. I saw within it the source of all love and all peace. While I was rising, I realized that I had just died. At that moment, I thought of my children and I said to myself, "Oh, my God, my children, what will they think of me? The very active mother I had been in their eyes never had time for them!" It was possible for me to see my life as it had really been, which saddened me. I left the house every day in order to change the world and I hadn't even been able to take care of my children.

During this time of emptiness I experienced because of my children, I saw something incredible: my body was no longer part of time-space. In an instant, I was able to visually embrace the whole world: the world of the living and the world of the dead. I was able to hug my grandparents and my deceased relatives. I was able to bring the whole world close to me: it was such a beautiful moment! I then understood that I had been duped into believing in reincarnation; I had become an advocate of it. I was used to "seeing" my grandfather and my great-grandfather everywhere. But now they were embracing me and I was among them. In one instant, I was holding and hugging all of the beings I had known in my life.

During these beautiful out-of-body moments, I had lost the sense of time. My outlook had changed. [On earth] I was always comparing myself with the obese person or the person of color or the ugly person because I held so many prejudices. While out of my body, I considered beings from the inside. It was so beautiful seeing people from the inside! I could understand their thoughts and feelings. I could embrace them all in one instant while continuing to lift myself up and becoming full of joy. I understood then that I would be gifted with a beautiful sight: a lake of extraordinary beauty. But at that moment, I heard the sound of my husband's voice; he was in tears, crying and calling out to me: "Gloria, please, don't leave me! Gloria, come back! Don't leave the children, Gloria." I then looked at him and not only did I see him, I felt his deep sadness. And the Lord allowed me to return even though it wasn't my wish. I was experiencing so much joy, peace, and happiness! And there I was, returning gently into my body where I was lying motionless. It was resting on a stretcher at the campus medical center. I could see the doctors who were giving me electroshocks and were attempting to resuscitate me following my cardiac arrest. We stayed there two and a half hours. At first, the doctors could not handle us because our bodies were still conducting electricity. Then, when they were able to touch us, they worked hard to try to bring us back to life.

I laid myself close to my head and I felt a shock that brought me violently back inside my body. It was painful because there were sparks everywhere. I saw myself reintegrate into something very small (my body). My dead and burned flesh was hurting terribly. They let out smoke and vapor. But for me there was another terrible pain: the vanity of a worldly woman, an enterprising woman, an intellectual; a student slave to her body, to beauty, and to fashion. I dedicated four hours every day to aerobics; enslaved to having a beautiful body. I underwent massages, diets, injections ... basically everything you can imagine. This was my life, a routine of slavery in order to have a beautiful body. I always used to say, "If I have beautiful breasts, they are to be shown. There is no reason to hide them." I said the same thing about my legs, because I knew I had spectacular legs and a beautiful chest! But in an instant, I saw with horror how my whole life had been only a continual and useless care of my body. Because this was the center of my life: love of my body. And now, I no longer had a body! In the place of the breasts I had startling holes, especially the left one, which was practically gone. The legs were a sight to be seen, like fragments, but without flesh, black as coal. They then brought me to the hospital where they operated on me immediately, and began to remove all the burned tissue.

While they were anaesthetizing me, I came out of my body again, worried about my legs. Then all of a sudden, in that same moment, something horrible happened. My whole life, I had been a "diet Catholic." My relationship with God was taken care of in a twenty-five-minute Sunday Mass, and that's all. I went to a Mass where the priest spoke less because I didn't want to put up with the anguish I felt with those priests who spoke a lot. This was my relationship with God. I was taken along by all of the worldly currents.

One day, when I was studying for the specialization, I heard a priest affirm that hell does not exist and that demons don't exist either. Unfortunately, my fear of the devil was my only tie to the church. When I heard that hell does not exist, I immediately told myself that if we all go to heaven, it is not important who we are or what we do. This caused me to move away from the Lord. I began to speak badly, using cusswords, etc. I no longer had any fear of sin, and I began to ruin my relationship with God. I started saying to everyone that the demons do not exist, that they are the inventions of the priests and manipulations of the church. I went to the point of saying to my colleagues at the university that God does not exist, that we are products of evolution. In that moment in the operating room, when I saw myself in that situation, I felt a terrible fright! I saw that the demons existed and that they were coming to present me with the bill, so to speak, since I had accepted their offers of sin! I began to see a great many people come out of the walls of the operating room. They appeared normal at first. In fact, they had a look full of hate—diabolic, frightening. I had a special moment of awareness: I understood, in fact, that to each one of these I owed something, that sin is not gratuitous, and that the principal lie of the devil is to say that he does not exist. I saw them all coming to surround me, to seek me! Just imagine the fright, the terror! My scientific and intellectual mind did not help me at all. I went around in the room; I was trying to get back into my body, but this flesh of mine did not receive me. I ended up fleeing as fast as I could. I passed through the wall of the operating room, hoping to be able to hide in the aisles of the hospital, but I ended up jumping into emptiness.

I headed toward a tunnel that pulled me down. At first, there was still a little light; it was as if I was in a beehive. There were so many people. I continued to descend, passing through more tunnels in a frightening darkness. I arrived to an obscurity that cannot be compared to anything else. I can only say that the darkest obscurity on earth is not even comparable; it's as if this would be like the full sunlight at midday. Down there, that same obscurity generates pain, horror, shame, and stinks terribly. It is a living obscurity; there the mind is dead or inert.

At the end of my descent, running along all these tunnels, I arrived to a level place. I was frantic, with a will of iron to get out of there; the same will that I had to take my life to new levels, but now it did not help me at all because I was there and I was going nowhere. At a certain point I saw the ground open up like a great mouth—it was enormous, a frightening abyss. That which chilled me the most was that, from there down, one could not feel even a fraction of the love of God, not even a drop of hope. That chasm had something that sucked me into it. I cried out like a mad woman, terrorized, feeling the horror of not being able to avoid that descent, because I realized that I was irretrievably sliding inside. I knew that if I were to enter, it would mean the spiritual death of my soul. But in this horror so great, precisely while I was about to enter, I was seized by the feet. My body entered in that abyss, but the feet remained held on high. It was a terrible moment and truly painful. My atheism disappeared as I began crying out to the souls of purgatory to pull me out of there. While I was crying out, I began to hear thousands and thousands of people crying, including youth, with so much suffering. I could see that there, in that horrible place, they were gnashing their teeth, with screams and laments that filled me with compassion and that I will never be able to forget. I still cry and suffer when I remember the suffering of all those people. I understood that this is the place where people go who, in a moment of desperation, committed suicide. But the cruelest of these torments was the absence of God, because there, one does not feel God.

In this suffering and anguish, I began again to cry out, "There must be a mistake! You see, I am a saint: I never stole, I never killed, I never did anything evil to anyone! On the contrary, I extracted and adjusted teeth; many times I did not require clients to pay if they were unable. I bought things and I gave them to the poor! What am I doing here? ... I went to Mass every Sunday ... I never missed Mass. If I missed Mass five times in my whole life, it was a lot! What is it that I am doing here? Pull me out of here! I am Catholic! I am Catholic, please, get me out of here!" When I shouted out that I was Catholic, I saw a faint light; a small light— even very small—in that darkness is the greatest gift that one can receive. I saw some steps at the top of this chasm, and I saw my father who had died five years before. Four more steps up I saw my mother, with much more light and in a position of prayer.

As soon as I saw them, I experienced a joy so great that I began to cry out, "Dad! Mom! Come and take me out of here! Please, get me out of here, I beg you!" When they looked toward me and they saw me there, you cannot imagine the immense pain that their faces revealed. In that place, we are able to perceive the sentiments of others; I saw that their suffering was so great. My father began to cry so, so much, and he cried out, "My daughter! Oh, no! My daughter!" My mother was praying ... and I understood with horror that they could not pull me out of there! When I saw this, I cried out again, desperate, "Take me out of here! I do not have cause to be here. I am Catholic! I beg of you, take me out of here!" This time, I heard a voice, so sweet and beautiful that it filled everything with peace and love and made my soul jump. Those horrible creatures that were clinging to me immediately asked permission to withdraw themselves because they could not stand the love in that voice. That voice, so beautiful, said to me. "Very well, if you are Catholic, tell me the commandments of the law of God!"

Think of the fright I experienced because I just did not expect that question. I only knew that there were Ten Commandments, and nothing more! I wondered how to cope with this. Then I remembered that my mother used to say that the first commandment was love. All I needed to do was repeat what she told me. I thought I could improvise and mask my ignorance. So I chose this answer, hoping that it would suffice and that the rest might not be noticed. I was thinking to get by in this way, as I always did when I was on earth. I always succeeded in justifying myself and in defending myself in such a way. I began to say, "The first commandment is to love God above everything else, and to love your neighbor as yourself." "Very well," he said to me, "and did you do this? Did you love?" I replied, "I … yes, I loved them! I loved them! I loved them!" But that wonderful voice said: "No!!! You did not love your Lord above all things, and even less did you love your neighbor as yourself! You made of yourself a god that you modeled on yourself, on your life! Only in moments of extreme necessity or in suffering, you remembered your Lord. And then yes, you knelt down when you were poor, when your family was humble, when you still desired to become a professional, then yes, every day you used to pray on your knees for long hours, beseeching your Lord to pull you out of that poverty, that I might permit you to become a professional and to be someone. When you found yourself in need of money, then yes, you promised. This was the relationship that you used to have with your Lord!"

I recognized that I took the rosary and I expected money in return; thus was my relationship with the Lord. Just as soon as he permitted me to have my profession and the associated prestige and money, I didn't have for him the least expression of love or gratitude. To be grateful? Never! Not even a "thank you" for the new day that he gave me, or for the health of my children, or for having a roof over my head. I was ungrateful to the max, with not a bit of compassion toward those in need! More than anything else, I became more incredulous in regard to my Lord, while I believed in Venus and Mercury for fortune. I went blindly after astrology, saying that the stars direct our life. I began to believe in all the doctrines that the world offered me. I believed, for example, in reincarnation: I convinced myself that I would die and begin again from the start ... and I forgot that it cost my Lord Jesus the price of blood. The Lord made me examine the Ten Commandments, showing me that the words I used to adore and love God were really in adoration of Satan. In my outpatients' clinic, a lady who read the cards would usually come do some magic in order to set people free from bad influences, and I used to say, "I do not believe in these things but do it anyway, because one never knows ..." In a corner where no one saw, she put a horseshoe and an aloe plant in order to keep away bad fortune.

You see that all this was so shameful. God made an analysis of my whole life in light of the Ten Commandments. He showed me how I was in relation to my neighbor. He also showed me how I pretended to love him while I criticized everything and everyone and while I pointed my finger at everyone, thinking of myself as "Holy Gloria." He showed me that I told others to love God and their neighbor, while I was a very envious and ungrateful person. I was never grateful to my parents for all their sacrifice and commitment to me so that I might have a profession and be able to thrive in life. As soon as I had my diploma, I found my parents to be inferior in my eyes, to the point that I was ashamed of my mother for her humility and poverty.

Jesus continued, showing me what kind of a spouse I was: I spent the whole day grumbling from when I awoke until I went to sleep. My husband would say, "Have a nice day," and I would reply, "Maybe it will be for you! I'm unhappy because of the rain." I always grumbled and contradicted everything, including my children. He showed me how I had no compassion for my brothers and sisters on earth. The Lord told me, "You have never considered the sick. In their solitude, you never offered them your company. You had no compassion for orphan children or all of the suffering children." I had a heart made of stone inside a hard shell. In the exam that Jesus gave me on the Ten Commandments, I saw how from greed came forth all my evils.

It was terrible, devastating! I felt completely capsized and I told myself, "At least, no one could blame me for having killed someone!"

For example, I paid the groceries at the supermarket for people in need, but I did not do it for love. I did it because I liked that all might see my gesture and that they might say I was good, that I was a saint. In fact, I would say, "I do this for you, but in exchange you do me a favor and go in my stead to my children's school, to the parent-teacher meetings, because I do not have time." In this way, I manipulated everyone. Moreover, I adored having lots of people at my feet, people who would say I was good and generous, or even a saint. I had fabricated a positive image of myself.

He said to me, "You had a god, and this god was money, and due to it you condemned yourself. Due to it, you sank into the abyss, and you went away from your Lord." I was blinded by this desire to have money, a lot of money, because I thought the more money I had, the more I would be happy. But in the end, we ended up being insolvent, without any money and paralyzed with debt. I felt alone, empty, bitter, frustrated.

When it came to the second commandment, I sadly saw that when I was still little, I learned that in order to avoid the severe punishments from my mother, I began lying. I formed an alliance with the "father of lies," that is, Satan, and I became such a great liar that my sins grew, increased in proportion with the lies. I knew, for example, that my mother had a great respect for the Lord. For her, the name of the Lord was sacred, it was most holy, so I thought I had the perfect weapon. I used to say to her, "Mom, in the name of Christ, I swear that I did not do this!" In this way I succeeded in avoiding my mother's punishments. With my lies, I implicated the most holy name of Christ.

Please note, brothers and sisters, that words are not in vain: When my mother didn't believe me, I said, "Mom, listen! If I am lying, may a lightning bolt come strike me!" These words I used many times. And you see! A lot of time has passed, but truly a lightning bolt ended up striking me and burned me to a crisp! And if I am here now, it is only because of the mercy of God.

I was shown how I believed myself to be a good Catholic woman but I did not respect any of my promises and I fruitlessly used the name of God. I was surprised to see that in the presence of the Lord, all those horrible creatures that had surrounded me bowed in adoration. I saw the Virgin Mary at the feet of our Lord; she was praying and interceding for me.

As for respecting the Day of the Lord, I was horribly irresponsible, and I suffered greatly because of it. I was told that on Sundays, I would spend four or five hours busying myself with care for my body. I could not even find ten minutes to spend praying or giving thanks for the Lord. In reciting the rosary, I would tell myself that I could do it during the ads so I would not miss a moment of the soap operas.

Jesus continued to show me how I was in no way grateful in regard to him, and the laziness that I had in going to Mass. When I still lived with my parents, and my mother obliged me to go, I said to her, "But, Mom, if God is everywhere, what need do I have to go to church for the Mass?" Jesus showed this to me: I had the Lord twenty-four hours a day—all my life God took care of me. Was I so lazy that I couldn't dedicate a little time to him on Sunday, to show him my gratitude, my love for him? But the worst thing was to know that, to frequent the church meant that I would nourish my soul. Instead, I dedicated myself totally to the care of my body. I became a slave to my flesh, and I forgot this in particular: that I had a soul and that it needed nourishment. Never did I nourish it with the Word of God, since I even said impudently that one who reads the Bible a lot becomes crazy.

Regarding the Sacraments, I was all wrong. I would say that I would never go to confession because those old priests were worse than me. The devil had me fooled about confession and that's how he kept my soul from being clean and from healing. The lily-white purity of my soul paid the price each time I sinned. Satan would leave his mark: a dark trace. All except for my first communion,

I never had a good confession. From then on, I couldn't receive the Lord with dignity. The lack of consistency in my life was so severe that I would blaspheme by saying, "But what Most Holy? Would God really exist in a mere piece of bread?" To what point did I arrive in degrading my relationship with God! I left my soul without nourishment, and as if that were not enough, I ended up constantly criticizing the priests. You wouldn't believe how much effort I put into it! From a tender age, my father had the bad habit of criticizing priests for being more womanizing than the laity. The Lord said to me, "Who are you to judge my anointed ones? They are of flesh, and the priest's sanctity is held by the community. The community must pray for him, love him, and support him. When a priest makes a mistake, his whole community is beholden to him—not he to himself." At a certain point, I declared a priest to be homosexual, and the whole community came to know this. You cannot imagine the evil that I did to that priest!

Jesus continued to show me the fourth commandment. I already recounted to you how I was ungrateful to my parents, how I was ashamed of them. I spoke bad about them and I disavowed them because they were poor and could not give me all that my rich friends had. I was an ungrateful daughter. I was ungrateful to the point of saying that I did not recognize my mother because she seemed inferior to me. The Lord showed me that I could have followed this commandment. In fact, I spent a lot of money on my parents because both of them had grave sicknesses before dying. The Lord showed me how I analyzed everything in terms of money. I manipulated even my parents when I had money and power; I even profited from them. Do you know what grieved me the most? To see my father crying, seeing that he had been a good father and taught his daughter to be a worker, a fighter, an entrepreneur. Yet he had forgotten an important thing: that I had a soul, and that he was my evangelizer. My life began to sink from his example. He was a womanizer, and he used to drink and smoke. When I was young and I saw my mother cry, I began to feel anger and rage.

Later, I began to say to my mother, "Mom, get separated from Dad, because it is impossible to put up with such a man! Have a little dignity, show him your worth." But my mother used to say, "No, my daughter, I cannot; I suffer, it is true, but I sacrifice myself for you, my children. You are seven and I am only one. I sacrifice myself because yours is a good father. I would be incapable of separating myself from him and leaving you without a father. And then, if I separated from him, who would pray so that your father might be saved? It is I that can beseech the Lord for him, so that he might find salvation. In fact, the pain and the suffering that he leaves me with, I unite them to the pains that Jesus suffered on the Cross. Every day I go to church, and before the tabernacle I say, "Lord, this suffering is nothing compared to your suffering on the Cross. Please be sure that my husband and my children might be saved." Still, I felt so much rage that I became a rebel. I began to live with the desire to defend the woman. I supported abortion, cohabitation, and divorce.

When the Lord invited me to look into the fifth commandment, he showed me the horrible assassin that I had been by committing the most terrible of crimes: abortion. Furthermore, I had financially helped many abortions because I believed that a woman had a right to choose whether she will be pregnant or not. I was told to read in the Book of Life and I was mortified to find that a fourteen-year-old girl had gone through an abortion under my counsel. I had equally counseled several girls, three of which were my nieces, by telling them about seduction, about the benefits of fashion, about using their bodies, and about protecting themselves with contraception. I was effectively corrupting minors, which added to the terrible sin of abortion.

Every time that the blood of a baby is scattered, it is a holocaust to Satan, who in this way acquires more power. I saw in the Book of Life how our soul is formed. The moment that the seed reaches the egg, a beautiful spark is ignited—it is a light that shines God the Father's eternal sunshine. There is a cry so great when they kill the soul during abortion, it devastates all of heaven. On the contrary, it is a cry of jubilation and of triumph in hell. How many babies are killed each day? It's a victory for hell. The price of this innocent blood is to liberate another demon each time. The devils soaked me in the blood of those babies that

I aborted or that I contributed in killing and my soul became completely black. After the abortions, I thought that I was free from sinning. Everything seemed OK to me. The saddest thing was to see what Jesus showed me: because I was using an IUD (intrauterine device) as a contraceptive, I was in essence preventing another life from happening. It's not surprising that I was always bitter, frustrated, and depressive. I was going deeper into the blackness of my soul. How could I even imagine that I had not killed anyone?

Moreover, the people who I did not like, who I hated and detested—I spoke badly about them. I was a false person, a hypocrite, and also an assassin, because it is not only with weapons that one kills a person. To hate, to slander, to envy, to deride, to do evil—this is also killing.

On the sixth commandment, I was still full of pride: I was always faithful to my husband! But the Lord showed me that I exhibited too much of my body. I went around with my breasts exposed and with my skintight stockings, I would make men look at me so they would admire me. But the Lord showed me that I was provoking them and that they sinned with me. Moreover, I counseled other women to commit adultery if their husbands had been unfaithful to them. I preached against forgiveness and I encouraged divorce. Jesus showed me, and I could see very well, how sins of the flesh are abominable and condemnable even if the modern world believes that it's okay to conduct ourselves like animals.

It was very sad to see how my father's sin and adultery did so much harm to us. My brothers became exact copies of my father. They became womanizers and they drank, not realizing the evil that they did to their own children. This is why my father was crying with great suffering, while in purgatory, seeing the consequences of his sins and of his example on his children.

As for the seventh commandment, to not steal, I said I had never stolen. I considered myself honest, but I stole from God. In my house, food was wasted, while in other houses of the world there was hunger. He said to me, "I was hungry, and look what you did with what I gave you—you wasted it. I was cold, and look what you did: you were a slave of fashion and of appearances; you bought brand-name goods and jewelry. You went to the point to spend lots of money on injections to be thin. You were a slave to your body to the point of making of it a god." Jesus showed how I was responsible for the hunger and for the conditions in my country and in the world. He showed me how, when I spoke badly about someone, I robbed him of his honor. He showed me that it was easier to give back stolen money, because one could give it back. But who can render a person's honor back to him? Also, I stole from my children the grace of having a mother at home, a tender and sweet mother who might have loved them. Instead, I would abandon them to the television, to the computer, and to video games. In order to satisfy my conscience, I would buy them brand-name clothing and everything that they wanted. How horrible! What a terrible chagrin!

In the Book of Life, we see everything as if in a movie. It was awful to see my children who were saying, "Let us hope that Mom arrives late! Let us hope that there will be a lot of traffic and she arrives later, because she is so boring, unpleasant, and when she arrives she always grumbles and shouts!" I stole the mother away from these babies; I robbed them of the peaceful home they deserved. I did not teach them to know the love of God and the love for one's neighbor by way of me. But I could not give what I did not have. If I do not love my neighbor, I cannot love the Lord, and if I do not have compassion, I am even less able to love the Lord.

Also, let me tell you, to lie is to steal. In this, I became an expert, because Satan became my father. In fact, you can have for a father God or Satan. There are no innocent lies. Lies are lies, and Satan is the father of lies. The sins of the tongue are terrible! I saw all the evil that I had done with my tongue when I criticized, when I derided, when I gave nicknames to someone. I saw how the nicknames I used to call a person must have hurt that person, creating a tremendous inferiority complex capable of destruction! For example, I called an obese woman "fat," making her suffer, and because of this, she ended up destroying herself.

God gave me an analysis of my whole life in light of the Ten Commandments. He showed me how all of my sins had to do with lust—that terrible of feelings. We had always been happy having a lot of money, and money became an obsession. It's really sad, because my soul's most challenging moments were those where I had a lot of money. I had even thought of suicide. This obsession with money made me turn away from the Lord such that I was no longer being cradled in his caring hands. After this examination of the Ten Commandments, the Lord showed me the Book of Life. I would like to be able to have the exact words to describe it.

My Book of Life began when my parents' cells were united in a loving embrace. In that instant of fecundation, there is like a spark of divine light, a beautiful explosion, and a soul is formed, my soul, created by the hands of God the Father. I discovered a God so beautiful, tender, and attentive, who cares for us twenty-four hours a day. He loved me and protected me; his love was my only punishment. He looked not at my flesh but at my soul, and he saw how I was distancing myself from salvation.

I was also shown how I was very hypocritical and harmful to others. For instance, I complimented a woman by saying, "You are pretty; what a nice dress, you look good in it!" But inside I was thinking, "How gross! You are ugly, and you believe yourself to be a queen!" In the Book of Life, you see all of your thoughts and judgments just as you thought them, because you can see inside the soul. All of my lies came to light, as if everyone could see them. How many times I snuck out of the house without my mother knowing, because she did not let me go anywhere. I invented lies to cover up: "Mamma, I have group work to do in the library." She believed me. Meantime, I went to see a pornographic film or to the bar to get a beer with my girlfriends. What shame I felt when I realized my mother could now see everything in the Book of Life!

At that time, my parents were very poor. My mother would give me a little milk and a banana or some guava paste to bring to school for lunch. I would eat the banana and then throw the peel wherever I happened to be; it never came to mind that someone could hurt themselves by slipping on the banana peel. I could have killed someone, with my recklessness and lack of mercy.

I saw, with great pain and shame, how I had an honest confession only once as an adult. It was when a lady gave me 4,500 pesos extra in change in a Bogotà supermarket. My father had taught us to be honest and to never touch even a penny of someone else's money. I figured out the error while in the car driving to my outpatient clinic, and I said to myself, "Oh, dear, that stupid person gave me 4,500 pesos too much! Now I must go back to the store!" But looking in the rearview mirror, I saw that there was a traffic jam, and I decided not to return to the store. But I had remorse for what I had done. The following Sunday, I went to confession and said, "I accuse myself of having stolen 4,500 pesos. Instead of giving the money back, I kept it for myself!" I did not even pay attention to what the priest said to me in reply. But the Lord said to me, "It was a lack of charity to not give the money back, because for you, 4,500 pesos was nothing, but for that woman it would have been three days' worth of food." The Lord showed me how that woman and her two babies went hungry for a couple of days due to my lack of awareness.

The Lord then asked me the following question: "What spiritual treasures do you bring to me?" Spiritual treasures? My hands were empty! So he said to me, "What use were those two apartments you had, the houses you possessed, and the outpatient clinics you ran if you can't even bring me a grain of sand? And you felt great satisfaction in your professional accomplishments? What have you done with the talents I gave you? You had a mission—to defend the Kingdom of Love, the Kingdom of God." Indeed, I had forgotten that I had a soul. Also, how could I remember that I had talents? All of the good deeds that I did know how to realize was of great hurt to the Lord.

The Lord then asked me to render an account for my lack of love and charity for my neighbor, and he said to me: "Your spiritual death began when you let yourself not be moved by suffering, and yet you too experienced it. You were alive, but you were really dead." If you could see what spiritual death is! A soul that hates is frightfully horrible; it is ugly, embittered, and disgusting; it is full of sin and hurts everyone. I saw mine as beautiful and sweet smelling. But inside was a tremendous stink and my soul had sunken into the abyss. This is why I was so depressed and bitter. The Lord said to me, "Your spiritual death began when you did not let yourself be sensitive to and compassionate for your neighbor. I warned you by showing you the tribulations of your neighbors everywhere, or you would hear the news about mass killings, about kidnappings, about the situation of refugees. You would say, "Oh, those poor people!" But in reality, you did not grieve and you did not feel anything in your heart. You had a heart of stone, and it was sin that made it so."

When my Book of Life was closed, imagine my sadness, my shame, my immense sorrow. I felt sorrow for God, my Father, to have behaved in such a way. Despite my behavior, my sins, my filth, my indifference, and my horrible feelings, the Lord sought me out even to the last instant. He always sent me people who had a positive influence on me. He let me fall into disgrace in order to seek me, and that I might seek him. He followed after me always, even to the last instant. He is a powerful God who begs next to each of us so that we might convert.

Clearly, I could not blame him for condemning me. In fact, of my free will I chose Satan as my father instead of God. When the Book of Life was closed, I noticed that I was headed for a deep well at the bottom of which there was a trap. While I was descending in this well, I began to call on all the saints in heaven to save me. Imagine all the names of saints that I recalled in that instant: a feat for a bad Catholic! I called on Saint Isidore or Saint Francis of Assisi, and when I exhausted my list, a deafening silence prevailed. I felt a terrible void and deep grief.

I thought that everyone on earth believed that I had died a beautiful death; maybe they were even ready to request an intercession on my behalf! And notice where I landed! I lifted up my eyes, and I met those of my mother. I felt so much sadness, a profound sorrow, because she would have wanted so much to carry me into the hands of God. With great confusion and suffering, I cried out to her: "Mamma, what a shame! I have been condemned! Where I am going, I will never see you again!" But in that moment, Jesus granted her a beautiful grace. My mother was motionless except that God facilitated her fingers pointing upward. As I looked, my eyes were very painfully liberated of some crust. In that instant, my spiritual blindness went away and I saw my life flash before my eyes. I saw that one day, one of my patients said to me, "Doctor, I feel lots of pain and sadness for you, because you are too much of a materialist. One day, if you find yourself in some affliction, ask Jesus Christ that he might cure you with his blood, because never will he abandon you, having paid the price of his own blood for you."

With great shame and immense sorrow, I began to cry out, "Lord Jesus Christ, have compassion on me! Forgive me, Lord, forgive me! Give me a second chance!"

The most beautiful moment of my life occurred right then. I do not have words to describe it. Jesus bent down and pulled me out of that pit! He lifted me and brought me to a level place, and he said to me with much love, "Yes, you will return, and you will have your second chance. I am not doing this because of the prayer from your family, because it is normal that they cry and vouch for you. I do this thanks to the intercession of all the people unrelated to your flesh and blood, that have cried, prayed, and lifted up their hearts with so much love for you."

I then saw the great power of the prayer of intercession. I saw how thousands and thousands of little flames lit up; they were little white flames full of love. They were the prayers of so many people who were praying for me. Among those little lights, there was an enormous and very beautiful one, a light much greater than all the others. I looked with curiosity in order to see who that person might be who loved me so much. The Lord said to me, "That man you see there is a person who loves you very much, and he does not even know you." He showed me that it was a poor peasant man, who lived in the mountains, in the Sierra Nevada de Santa Marta [in northeastern Colombia]. This man was very poor; he hardly had anything to eat. He went to church and then went to buy a piece of blue soap [washing soap]; it was wrapped in a piece of newspaper from the day before. There was the news of my accident and a photograph where I appeared totally burned. When this man saw the news, he prostrated with his face to the ground and beseeched

God with all his heart, saying, "Father, my Lord, have compassion on my little sister, save her, save her, Lord! Lord, if you save her, if you save my little sister, I promise you to go to the "Sanctuary of Buga" [in the southwest of Columbia]. Please, Lord, save her!"

Think about it: He was such a poor man who never cursed nor lamented his hunger. On the contrary, he had such a great capacity for love that, even with having little to eat, he offered to cross the country in order to fulfill a promise, in favor of someone he did not even know! The Lord said to me, "It is like this that you must love your neighbor." And it was there that he gave me this mission: "You will go back [to earth] to give your testimony and you will repeat it not a thousand times but a thousand times a thousand. Woe to those who, after listening to you, will not change, because he will be judged with greater severity. This applies also to you upon your second return, and it applies for the religious ones who are my priests as well. There is no greater deaf person than the one who does not want to hear!"

This testimony, my dear brothers and sisters, is not a threat. On the contrary, the Lord does not need to threaten us. This is a second chance that I was granted, thank God, and it is also for you. When your hour arrives to leave this world, each one of you will also be presented with your own Book of Life. All of this will pass before your eyes just as it did for me. There, we will see ourselves exactly as we are now, with the only exception that we will also see our thoughts, our sentiments, and our actions—all in the presence of God. The most beautiful thing is that each one of us will see the Lord face to face, asking us to convert ourselves so that we may be new creatures with him, because without him, we could not do it! May the Lord bless everyone immensely.

Glory to God!

Glory to Our Lord Jesus Christ.

Spiritual death is a loss of the state of grace.

Gloria Polo[4]

Three Citations

No one can generate a life for himself. It is from life itself that another life arises, even when the life of an embryo is manipulated through an in vitro technique. Life never comes from nowhere. Whether one is created through an act of love, which is most humane, or whether one is created in a test tube, it is from an already existing life that another life, our life, emerges. Life reveals itself through a living creature that provides its support and expression. Since life engenders its own self in a living creature within which it expresses itself, and since not one of these creatures has given itself life, we can conclude that, in going to the origin of life, there is necessarily "a Life capable of engendering itself, that which Christianity calls God."⁵

It is thus that in Christianity, the auto-generated Life is the Father, and the Living Creature that is eternally engendered and that expresses Life is the Word or perhaps the Son.⁶

—Michel Aupetit

The great truths of traditional religions are being reinforced by this notion. Indeed, life continues immediately after death and without interruption. Indeed, there is a better life for those who have known how to share their love with others. Indeed again, those who devoted themselves to an egotistical, fanatical life will need to go through a slow and often painful transformation to learn to love themselves. Still, we are all finally awaited for, sustained, and helped by the Love that is at the root of our very existence. This is the greatest discovery of those who have lived such experiences: the infinite love of God.

—François Brune

[Yes, I do think that NDEs] give a new perspective of life and suggest that, perhaps, it is not as arbitrary or as absurd as many postmodern thinkers feel it is. In this respect, NDE gives rise to a wholly different set of values for living than those that currently dominate our culture. It suggests that perhaps some of the teachings of the spiritual traditions and the universal parts of religious traditions still have relevance in these times after all.

—Kenneth Ring

Anthropological Approach

Because the spiritual is in itself carnal.
    —Charles Péguy

In order to interpret what essentially happens during a near-death experience, we need to rely on a practical anthropology. Whatever the case, the existence of NDEs is unthinkable without accepting the reality of the soul (which scientists prefer to call "consciousness," a general term that remains not clearly defined) and its connection with human existence.

These days, the soul seems to be interpreted as a fabrication of religious doctrines. It is no longer seen as an extension of the psyche. The individual is primarily considered to be a psychosomatic entity: the combination of body and psyche. For about one hundred and fifty years, science has applied itself to this erroneous dualism, which has happened alongside the beginnings of modern psychology and psychoanalysis, the discovery of the unconscious, and all of the explorations of the human sciences.

In fact, we shall see that the human being is both body and soul, the latter having a spiritual dimension that the scriptures refer to as the *heart* or the "spiritual heart" (the heart and spirit being considered two realities that are equivalent or close to one another[1]), centered in the soul.

Philosophical Approach

From a rational standpoint, it is possible to make a number of assertions deriving from a certain conception of the human being:

1. Our Bodies Change Continuously

From the very beginning, we are not the same at age one as we are at age seventy. What remains most constant is the face, which best expresses a person's inner nature. Biologically speaking, throughout our existence, five hundred thousand cells die and are reborn every second. About fifty billion cells are replaced each day in our bodies. Each year, about 98 percent of the molecules and atoms in our bodies are replaced. From this, we can conclude that we have a "new" body each year of our earthly existence.

Finally, the body—the only visible part of our being—is therefore in a perpetual process of transformation. It is in a constant unstable equilibrium between two opposing processes: disintegration and permanent reintegration,[2] until it completely decomposes at death. No one really thinks about this constant change.

2. A Body Cannot Exist without a Soul

If indeed I am always the same—today as I was yesterday or as I was five, ten, or seventy years ago—what then grants me the conscious ability to believe myself to be myself all the time? From where comes the constancy of this body that is perpetually changing? What helps maintain the integrity and constancy of my body?

There must be "something" that helps this along!

This "something"—this substantial entity that collects matter from multiple sources to form an organized and living body—has been called the "soul" (from Old English *sawl*) since Aristotle.[3] Whatever name we give it, the soul is a fact of life. It is not optional, it is not a different perspective on the spirit, and it is not an invention. Nonetheless, it is also astonishingly not verifiable and it evades all scientific investigation.

Still, from experience—and through a rational, logical, verifiable, and renewable analysis of experiential evidence—there truly exists *a support for the body and a cohesive strength that is present throughout a person's life*: What could it be if not the soul? *The soul is inherently linked to the body*. If there was no soul, there would be no body. It is the soul that makes the body a body and not just a grouping of atoms and molecules. As the French philosopher Claude Tresmontant says: "He who thinks the contrary, who would pretend to deny the existence of the soul, would be obliged to also believe that, instead of an organized, informed, individualized biological system it is but a heap, a heap of atoms. Never will a ton of atoms win the Nobel Prize!

"A body does not exist and cannot exist without a soul or without animation or without information—these expressions are synonyms. The body is an informed unit while the cadaver is an uninformed multiplicity," continues Tresmontant with much realism.[4]

3. The Soul Is Vital

The soul therefore sustains the power of life; it is animator and organizer of the body and it makes the subject *be*. It is the *principle of life*,[5] physical and psychical, that individualizes a living organism, which in return individualizes it.

Let us also note that, paradoxically, it is the soul—which is invisible to the senses—that is always true to its own self throughout life, whereas the body—which manifests as flesh and blood—is constantly renewed and in some ways becomes a "manifestation" of the soul.

Here is a logical conclusion: The soul is what makes a body a living body; *the soul is the body's life.* The soul does not superimpose itself on the body; it constitutes the body. *The soul is "animator" of the body.*[6] It is the living unit of the elements that make it up. The soul and the body are one. To prove this, think of what is left when we die. A body? No! A body that no longer contains its formative principle, that no longer has its vital energy that made it subsist. The body in its subjective form dies, is corrupted, and decomposes. All that is left is the matter of which it was made, a heap of molecules, a heap of atoms that no longer has life and that inevitably decomposes and returns to dust.

Matter does not live. An organism is what lives. The body is what lives. If not, it is no longer a body but rather an appearance of a body—an illusion of a body! A nonliving body is no longer a body; it is a cadaver, a relic, which is totally different.

4. The Soul Is the Seat of the Personality

With the soul, the person becomes conscious of himself as someone responsible for his actions, free to choose and to make decisions, and given the means to bring them to bear. These means are the usual human competencies—intelligence, reasoning, will, memory, imagination, affect. Through one's will, a person consents or refuses and then decides.

Through one's intelligence, he reasons in a deductive way. Affect is the seat of feelings, emotions, attractions, and repulsions.

In short, the psyche-soul is the overarching principle of man's embodied life. It is the conscious "I" he has of himself and of all his abilities and aptitudes.[7]

5. The Soul Is Spiritual

Everything alive is a soul—animals included, of course—and dependent on the corporeality with which it is linked. For the human being, it is not only corporeal but also immaterial, spiritual, and able to embody God's love.

Man, in fact, is not only limited to the material world. He senses, from the beginning, that he is not only matter. He is mystery. By nature, he is always drawn to search for something else. We very well know, from personal experience at least, that we are not just a digestive tube, or an inhaling and exhaling lung, or a sexual beast, or even a psyche moved by his fantasies. There is in us a yearning for good, for beauty, and for reality. There is no conscious human being who does not seek to know the meaning of his life, who does not yearn to be loved and to love, who does not wonder about his finitude.

From time immemorial, man has also been *homo religiosus* (religious man). History has taught us that there has been no civilization without religion. Nor has there been any civilization that, under one form or another, has not postulated the immortality of the soul. This intuition acts as an anchor for life's hopefulness. The human being therefore *inherently has a spiritual dimension that is integral to his nature.* His soul is also spiritual. We can call this spiritual soul "heart" or "spirit," from the Latin *spiritus*, which means "breath" (in Greek, *pneuma*).[8] It is the *spiritual heart.*

The spiritual heart is the *spiritually transcendent principle.* It cannot be reduced to the objects and forces of this world; it is the *elemental aspect* of the spiritual life of man. It is at the threshold of all that is divine—the threshold of our spiritual consciousness and of God's consciousness. *It is this infinite point at the center of the person—a place of bounty, of communion; a place where God's presence can be appreciated* through the gifts of belief, prayer, and adoration. It is not subjected to time or space, yet it makes us be present for—and brothers and sisters to—all of humanity in space and time.

Each of our hearts is called to open itself to be the Lord's temple.

6. Man Is a Vital and Spiritual Soul

There is an absolutely fundamental dimension of human existence, a superior dimension that distinguishes it from all other living creatures: the human body-soul composite is inspired. We know quite well that man is not a pure spirit—he is not an angel!—he is *a spiritual soul. Man is a psychosomatic spiritual being.*[9]

In fact, the human soul evades the organic death of the human body. It is immortal, yet it keeps the individuality (and history) of the body that it has inhabited. It remains a soul linked to its body.

7. The Body Is Spiritual

According to what we have already explored, it is important to admit that the body is also spiritual. We do not have a body; we are our own body. Our body is a human body and therefore a spiritual body. It is inseparable from our human condition. The body is our self. *The body is, in man, the primary morphology of the spirit and it is its permanent epiphany.*[10] The corpse is handled with a burial that is meant to respect and maintain our memory of the human body, a meaningful process for those who have known and loved the deceased person.[11]

In the end, it is important to remember that the soul is a central concept vitally linked with spirit. There are two sides to the soul, the spiritual side, which we call the "spiritual soul" and which gives life (and spirituality) to the body through its corporeal side or "corporeal soul." The body is alive and spiritual thanks to the soul, which is also alive and spiritual thanks to the spirit. All this combines into one. A human being is essentially *one*—body, soul, and spirit, with each one of these structures having an effect on the others.

Christian Approach

Christian anthropology does not deny any of this. Man is not made of an essentially heterogeneous composition. He is in part material (the body, which is external and visible) and in part spiritual (the soul, which is internal and invisible). This is a dualist, Neoplatonic conception. Christianity has always defended the fundamental and ontological unit of the human being, made of a body, a soul, and a spirit, with the soul (or "heart") at the center and uniting it all. In the *Catechism of the Catholic Church* (CCC), there is no "anthropological" entry, though the conception of the human being is essentially described in paragraph 6. This paragraph relates to the creation of man (especially sections 362 to 368); it is titled "Body and Soul but Truly One," where the soul essentially serves as the "spiritual principle" of the human being.[12]

The soul is equally the "vital principle." In segment 363, it says, "In Sacred Scripture the term *soul* often refers to human life" (see Matthew 16:25–26, John 15:13), and in section 367, "Sometimes the soul is distinguished from the spirit: St. Paul for instance prays that God may sanctify his people 'wholly,' with 'spirit and soul and body' kept sound and blameless at the Lord's coming" (1 Thessalonians 5:23).[13] By making this distinction, we can demonstrate that life is sacred because it is stakeholder of the spiritual.

In section 368, it clearly states that, "The spiritual tradition of the Church also emphasizes the *heart*, in the biblical sense of the 'depths of one's being' [Jeremiah 31:33], where the person decides for or against God."[14] In this case, in fact, the word *heart* rejoins the word *spirit* and allows a distinction (without needing to separate) the *vital soul*.[15]

Let us look at what is said in the *YouCat: Youth Catechism of the Catholic Church*, which was written in 2011 for the World Youth Day in Madrid. In the corresponding paragraphs to the above, speaking of the human creature in segments 56 to 63, it is said that, "Unlike inanimate objects, plants, and animals, man is a person endowed with a spirit" (section 58).[16] It is also very important to remember that, "The soul causes the material body to be a living human body" (section 62).[17]

The Christian faith says that at the end of times, we will resuscitate in body and soul. The soul, which will have become totally spiritual, will incarnate into a "spiritual body," a "glorious body," which cannot be corrupted, compared with our "animate body," which is corruptible. Our carnal body, which is already spiritual in more ways than one, will then become completely spiritual. The Christian faith supports a hopeful and faithful reality that goes well beyond the notion of the soul's immortality.[18]

From there, we must admit the factual incompatibility between reincarnation and resurrection. Indeed, these two beliefs give primacy to the spiritual order of things, and they are inhabited by a certain hope. Still, as theologian Father Bernard Sesboüe pointedly explains, "Reincarnation does not offer the body salvation, since the latter is but an interchangeable container; reincarnation can be comprehended within the dualism of body and soul."[19]

Near-Death Experiences

This anthropological approach perfectly confirms what we have already said: NDEs are a reanimation and in no way can they be a "resurrection" in the proper sense of the word; that is, a return of ontological death, which can only be definitive for common mortals. Jesus's resurrection is the only true one. (See various scriptural stories relative to this topic.) Jesus's resurrection was not the reanimation of his corpse, nor was it his return to temporal life. It was an extraction from our mortal condition and an entrance into the immaculate world of God.[20]

There are indeed three *returns to life* as reported in the Gospel: the daughter of Jairus, the son of Naim's widow, and Lazarus.[21] These are very special cases: these three people were in fact allegedly dead; their spiritual soul had already separated from their body.[22] This is not a case of resurrection but of *reanimation in the proper sense of the word, that is, a new linking of the spiritual principle to the body due to a miraculous intervention by Christ.* These events did not exist in NDEs either; they were indeed dead. There was a metaphysical death, an exodus, and a provisional return of the *spiritual soul* in the person (who will die later). It is most assuredly of a *miraculous* nature because it would be absolutely impossible otherwise.

In terms of the Virgin Mary, we speak of her Assumption (or of her Dormition, for the Orthodox Church). In fact, due to her Immaculate Conception (through which she was kept from original sin), the end of her life was described as an ascent to heaven, body and soul.

In NDEs, even when there is a phenomenon of disembodiment, there is no real, ontological separation between the spiritual soul (as the unique spiritual principle) and the physical body: if that were the case, we would speak of a "metaphysical death." In fact, it is inadmissible: It is impossible for the [spiritual] soul to leave the body and return to it later, since the separation is irreversible.[23]

For the human person, death is a seismic event that bursts apart his ontological unity. We can foresee that in this moment at the edge of death—between clinical death and definitive death—a kind of detachment between the body and the soul occurs. This detachment leads toward an inevitable separation, but it can still be reversed. It is within this period of time that the experiencers of NDEs report experiencing these phenomena.

Nonetheless, once a person reaches definitive death, he clearly crosses the threshold into the afterlife, that which we call eternal life. This life after death is no longer a process; according to Father Marin Panhard, former chaplain of the Notre-Dame de Montligeon sanctuary in La Chapelle-Montligeon, France, it is *an achievement where all of life is presented to us in an instant, an eternal instant, and where the very notion of time no longer exists.*[24]

Through this realistic anthropology, NDEs can be accepted and understood, and in return, they help to confirm this approach to understanding them.

> Yet God raised Jesus to life! God's Spirit now lives in you, and he will raise you to life by his Spirit (Romans 8:11).

—◦◦◦—

SIXTH TESTIMONY

"Shot!"

Here is a letter written by the Abbot Jean Derobert, a certified testimony offered in light of the canonization of Padre Pio.[1] Father Derobert, who is recently deceased, wrote a book regarding the life of this saint, *Padre Pio, transparent de Dieu* (Padre Pio, God's transparency).

Dear Father,

You requested a written summary on the topic of the protection with which I was gifted in August 1958, during the war in Algeria.

At the time, I was a member of the health services corps in the Army. I had noticed that, at each key moment of my life, Padre Pio—who had adopted me as his spiritual son in 1955—would send me a card letting me know that he was supporting me and praying for me. This was the case during my exam at the Gregorian University in Rome. This was also the case when I left for the army. And it was still the case when I had to join the troops in Algeria.

One night, a commando of the FLN (Algerian National Liberation Front) attacked our village. I was immediately restrained and placed in front of a door with five other soldiers; and that's where we were shot. I remember that I didn't think of my father or my mother—for whom I was an only child—but I was experiencing a great amount of joy because I was "going to see what was on the other side." I had received, that very morning, a card from Padre Pio with two handwritten lines: "Life is a constant struggle but it leads to the light" (underlined two or three times).

I immediately had the experience of a disembodiment. I saw my body next to me, fallen and bloodied in the midst of my comrades, who were also dead. I began a curious ascension through a kind of tunnel. Many known and unknown faces emerged from the fog that surrounded me. At first, these faces were somber; they were faces of people who did not have such a good reputation, sinners lacking in virtue. As I went up, the faces I saw became more luminous.

I was astonished to find out how I could walk … and I told myself that, in my mind, I was already outside of time, I had resurrected. I was able to see all around me without turning around.… I was also surprised that I was not feeling any of the wounds inflicted by the bullets that were shot at me … and I understood that they had entered my body so fast that I was able to hardly feel anything.

Suddenly, my thoughts turned to my parents. I immediately found myself at my house in Annecy, in my parents' room, where they were sleeping. I tried to talk to them, but alas, they could not hear me. I visited the apartment and noted the different placement of a piece of furniture. Many days later, while writing my mother, I asked her why she had moved the furniture. She answered in reply, "How do you know this?"

I thought of Pope Pius XII, who I knew well while I was a student in Rome. I found myself in his room, where he had just gone to bed. We spoke through the exchange of thoughts, since he was very spiritually attuned.

I pursued my ascension up to the point where I found myself in a beautiful scenery wrapped in a soft blueish light.… There was no sun, "since the Lord is their light," as it is said in Revelation. I saw thousands of people, all at about thirty years old, but I met a few of them who I had known when they were alive.… One of them died at the age of eighty … and she looked as if she was thirty.… Another died at the age of two … and she was the same age as the others.…

I left this "paradise" with many extraordinary flowers that I had never known down below. I went even higher.… There, I lost my human nature and I became a "drop of light."

I saw many other "drops of light" and I knew that one of them was Saint Peter, another was Paul or John or an apostle or a saint....

Then, I saw Mary in her full radiance and beauty; she met me with her ineffable smile.... Jesus was behind her, looking spectacularly beautiful. And behind them was an area of light that I knew was the Father, and I dove head on into it....

There, I felt a total fulfillment of everything I could ever have desired.... I experienced perfect happiness ... and briskly, I found myself back on earth with my face in the dirt and in the middle of my comrades' bloodied bodies.

I realized that the door in front of which I had stood was riddled with holes from the bullets that had gone through my body. My clothing was pierced and full of blood. My chest and my back were smudged with semi-dried but still viscous blood ... but I was intact. Looking like this, I went to see the commander. He came to me and cried a miracle. It was Commander Cazelle, who is now deceased.

This experience marked me for life, of course. But when I was liberated from the army, I went to Padre Pio, who had appeared from a distance in Saint-Francis hall. He asked me to come closer and offered me, as usual, a small sign of affection. He then told me these simple words: "Oh! You really took me for a ride this time! But what you saw, it was really beautiful, wasn't it?" And he stopped at that.

One can understand now why I'm no longer afraid of death ... since I know what lies ahead.

—Abbot Jean Derobert

Two Witnesses

Bishop Oscar Romero

Oscar Romero, bishop of San Salvador, had always advocated for the poor. Shortly before his assassination on March 24, 1980, while he was celebrating the Mass, he said, "If I am killed, I will resuscitate among the people; I say it without any boastfulness and with the greatest of humility. If someone succeeds in killing me, I forgive and bless the person or people who do it. I do not believe myself to be worthy of God's gift of martyrdom. But if God accepts the sacrifice of my life, may my blood sow the seeds of liberty and be a sign of hope."

Martin Luther King Jr.

In the last paragraph of his sermon on April 3, 1968, he said, "Well, I don't know what will happen now. We've got some difficult days ahead. But it really doesn't matter to me now, because I've been to the mountaintop. And I don't mind. Like anybody, I would like to live a long life. Longevity has its place. But I'm not concerned about that now. I just want to do God's will. And he's allowed me to go up to the mountain. And I've looked over. And I've seen the Promised Land. I may not get there with you. But I want you to know tonight, that we, as a people, will get to the Promised Land! And so I'm happy tonight. I'm not worried about anything. I'm not fearing any man! Mine eyes have seen the glory of the coming of the Lord!"

The next day, April 4, 1968, Martin Luther King Jr. was assassinated.

Other Extraordinary Phenomena

*In order to experience everyday spirituality, we need to remember that
we are spiritual beings spending some time in a human body.*
  —Barbara De Angelis

In order to better understand what happens during a near-death experience, we need to look at certain phenomena that are just as intriguing—and Christian—that it is interesting to compare them.

The Extraordinary Supernatural

There is a Christian supernatural, but it has been disparaged since we must admit that it is not always easy to find reasonable explanations for it. The church itself is extremely careful and vigilant in regards to this supernatural, because it does not want faith to rely on the extraordinary (at the risk of promoting fideism).

That is what theologian Father René Laurentin supports when he says:

> The extraordinary is rather poorly considered today, both in the scientific world as well as in the Catholic Church, and for different reasons.
>
> For the sciences, the "extraordinary" has little status. It is but an interference with accidental and incredible causes. These causes must be identified beyond the myths and the imaginary projections that they evoke in popular opinion. The unusual will never succumb to reason. The unexplained can never be inexplicable. It must be explained using the determinism of the causes and thus restored within the general order of things. The qualitative needs to be a subset of the quantitative; the splendor of the

spectrum of colors is reduced to the frequency of optical waves; the magic of concerts to the number of auditory vibrations; and of course, thinking is reduced to the brain's activity.[1] According to the scientific method, there is no *deus ex machina*; the insights that enlighten us are the result of quantifiable causes.

The extraordinary is not seen in a better light within the church. The latter is apprehensive of the illuminism of its enthusiastic believers and the projections of the imagination. It is always quick to objectify their desires, their aspirations, and their beliefs, while faith is a belief in the Word of God without sight: "Blessed are those who have not seen and yet have believed," says Jesus (John 20:29). Christian visions and prodigies are but added benefits that are modestly, marginally, and conjecturally discerned without ever reaching certainty. The church does not cultivate miracles; it doubts them, marginalizes them, and more often than not, speaks of them like annoying interferences or buffers keeping us at a distance from faith and the Sacraments. Thus, the church is heiress to the Bible and, as such, it has taken on the demythologization of the entire world: Yahweh's revelation ("I am") has destroyed all the myths of antiquity. And the Roman Empire condemned Christians as atheists because they annulled all religious myths.[2]

To rigorously approach the topic of these extraordinary phenomena requires us to reflect on the concept of the supernatural since the word *supernatural* is all too often confused for what is "marvelous." The supernatural is conversion, sanctification, and divinization. It is God's action that, by transforming nature, elevates it toward him. The supernatural is not an abstract moment to be superimposed on nature or on the domain of extraordinary phenomena. *It is at once what God invites in us (to live the Trinitarian life) and what he proposes will help us reconnect with him (the baptismal life in accordance with the Gospel),* according to Patrick Sbalchiero.[3] He also claims, with good reason, that, "The supernatural is never abstract, independent of concrete realities…. The extraordinary supernatural is not indispensable to Christian faith; the theological virtues suffice…. The extraordinary supernatural does not force people to believe."[4]

Historian Patrick Sbalchiero emphasizes two important points:

1. The supernatural refers to the order of grace, that is, the sanctification (or divinization for Easterners) of man through the Holy Spirit's bestowal. The supernatural is God's current and reasonable way of making himself manifest: through faith, the scripture, and theological instruction.
2. But there is a supernatural that is extraordinary, peripheral, and marginal. It shows up in the finer manifestations of God's presence.… The presence of the extraordinary in this world has only one reason to exist: that is to modestly invite us humans to see what God's creation has been called to become.

The Christian Extraordinary

The Christian extraordinary is the topic of choice when we compare NDEs—extraordinary phenomena, if any—with three kinds of singular Christian supernatural phenomena: apparitions, some mystical manifestations, and miracles.

1. Apparitions

Apparitions have existed throughout the church's history, and they seem to have increased in frequency, especially as concerns Marian apparitions. The church might recognize but does not become dogmatic in its interpretation: a Christian person is free to believe in it if he wishes.

The term *apparition* is used to designate an observation that is not usually visible. Aside from the criteria used to discern and recognize these extraordinary phenomena, what is most interesting to note are the possible mechanisms involved in their existence.

The most well-known apparitions have clearly indicated that the seers are usually in *ecstasy*. This particular kind of state cannot be acquired voluntarily; the seers are gifted with it in an altered state of consciousness. During the ecstatic state, the seers are not sleeping or dreaming, nor are they in an epileptic attack (which can provoke visions). Electroencephalograms register a diffuse and synchronous alpha rhythm throughout the brain. The seer's eyes are riveted on the apparition and are not blinking, indicating any kind of threat. There seems to be a general lack of sensitivity—to pain, in particular—as well as a lack of corneal sensitivity and an absence of neurological reflex. Finally, when the seers experience a group apparition, they seem to exhibit a similar demeanor.[5] These results imply anything but imitation or fraud, nor do they involve epilepsy or hallucination. They put an end to neurologist Dr. Jean-Martin Charcot's secular theory pertaining to which apparitions are phenomena resulting from hysteria.

The body is therefore no longer the same; it is no longer in its ordinary state. During the apparition, it seems the body no longer depends only on the vital soul but primarily on the spiritual soul, which allows it to *see the invisible.*

This is also what happens during mystical ecstasies (where people talk of "rapture"): the body takes on properties of a spiritual dimension.

During a Marian apparition, some seers have had a vision of the afterlife. This demonstrates that, much like with NDEs, a detachment of body, soul, and spirit is possible at least for a short time period. It was the case with the three seers of Fatima (in 1917 in Portugal).[6]

2. Mystical Manifestations

In some ways, mystical manifestations demonstrate the existence of the soul at the juncture between the spiritual and the corporeal.

The mystics are men or women who have most often chosen a monastic or a religious life, leaving behind the mundane to be entirely devoted to God. In this state of offering of self and of divine union, *their soul is so spiritualized* that "it is no longer them who is living but Christ who is living in them" (Galatians 2:20). Subsequently, some people can experience extraordinary manifestations without even seeking them.[7] These experiences, which can be called *mystical*, are a kind of approach to life liberated from materiality—a harbinger of things to come for those who live a life of goodwill.

Levitation is a kind of ecstatic ascending. Unexpectedly and in a moment's notice, the person's body rises from the ground—to a more or less high level and for an undetermined period of time—during a mystical contemplation (or rapture). There is an astonishing number of saints who have experienced this phenomenon and whose levitation was witnessed by a number of people. The only plausible explanation is that the spiritualized soul can draw the body with it; the body then loses its normal weightiness and can accomplish things that cannot happen under normal conditions.

Mystics can often also find themselves in two different locations at the same time. This incredibly surprising event is called a *bilocation*. This is not a movie; this has indeed occurred in the twentieth century with Mother Yvonne-Aimée of Malestroit (1901–1951)[8] and with Padre Pio (1887–1968).[9] The person remains in ecstasy in one location while doing normal activities in another place. The soul is the only probable thing that can be in two places at the same time.

The *stigmata* are "a kind of painful impression of Jesus's crucifixion wounds on people's hands, feet, forehead, and side of body, whether in ecstasy or not."[10] Saint Francis of Assisi was the first well-known stigmatized person in 1224. Since his time, over 350 stigmatized people have been identified, most of which have been mystics. The most recent and most notable of them are Thérèse Neumann (1898–1962), Padre Pio, Yvonne-Aimée of Malestroit, and Marthe Robin (1902–1981). We are led to believe that the soul is impregnated with God and with God made flesh in Jesus Christ—who died crucified on the cross—such that it manifests itself in the flesh.

With *inedia*, the mystic can live for a while without food. It was the case with Marthe Robin, who lived for a number of years by eating only the sacramental bread. We can imagine that her soul had enough nourishment to keep her body alive.

It is clear that modern medicine does not know how to explain the origin or the progression of these facts. For example, the stigmata never get infected nor do they result in inflammation or suppuration; the reparation of the flesh is abnormally fast even without any medical treatment; inedia and transverberation of the heart are outstanding phenomena. It is important to note also that the church canonized these people for their evangelical virtues and not for the atypical phenomena they experienced.

It is also good to understand that many mystics from all eras have undergone experiences with striking similarities to NDEs. That is the case with Catherine of Siena (1347–1380), Saint Mary Magdalene de Pazzi (1556–1607), Saint Teresa of Avila (1515–1582), Anne Catherine Emmerich (1774–1824), etc.

I will only rely on the example of Mary of Jesus Crucified, "the little Arab," now Saint Mariam Baouardy, whose incredible story of NDE is in the epilogue.

She was a practical, grounded woman; she was not "enlightened." Nonetheless, she consistently experienced the supernatural as she benefited throughout her life from a great number of extraordinary mystical manifestations, most of which were rarely associated with a single person: apparitions, visions, revelations, prophecies, ecstasies, miraculous healings, bilocation, stigmata, levitations, transverberation of the heart,[11] etc.

She had frequent ecstasies during which nothing or no one could make her budge; she was completely insensitive to anything and everything.

She had eight documented levitations at the Carmel of Pau (in France) in 1873.[12] People witnessed her ascending by the tips of branches of great linden trees all the way to the top of the tree in the blink of an eye. Once at the top, she would balance herself on a very small branch, too small to hold her physical weight, and praise God's love through song. Then, when her superior would order her, she would quietly descend, and once back in her body, she remembered nothing.

She had stigmata, first in her heart at age twenty, then on her forehead and in her hands. She did everything she could to not reveal them.

She experienced a transverberation in 1868 at the Carmel of Pau (at the hermitage of Our Lady of Mount Carmel in France).[13] This phenomenon was revealed after her death, and her heart was kept in Pau with a clearly visible sign of the transpiercing.[14]

She experienced many apparitions of angels, of Elijah, of Saint Joseph, of the Virgin Mary, and of Jesus![15] She singularly fought against Satan (in particular during a forty-day battle at the Carmel of Pau, from July 26 to September 4, 1868).

How can we explain all these extraordinary facts? Classical science will never be able to explain or reproduce these events.[16] I decided to mention them because they demonstrate how little we in fact know about human beings. The human soul is so much more profound than we can imagine. Within certain conditions, it can bring incredible possibilities to the person who is open to them!

3. Miracles

The numerous testimonies coming out of Lourdes since 1858—many of which I reported on in my last book[17]—clearly show certain similarities between NDEs and miraculous healings.

Miracles, like NDEs, are "signs" based on the testimonies of those who have experienced them.

Near-death experiences are often considered a kind of miracle by those who return from these experiences, especially following a violent "death." It is their testimony that counts, but let us remember that—must it be stated again?—clinical death is not a definitive death, so we are therefore not talking about a miracle in the strict sense of the word. Near-death experiences and miracles still have something in common: in NDEs, there is usually an encounter with a spiritual being that must be God, and in miracles, we talk of an extraordinary phenomenon that can be interpreted as resulting from a divinely inspired intervention.

It is troubling to note that NDEs—much like miracles—transform those who experience them, which in turn causes profound changes in one's understanding of life and death, with a real opening to the other. In both cases, this change comes from the meeting with the "spiritual being." They will never forget this meeting! It is good to note also that those who have experienced these phenomena usually do not try to convince others of their experience. If we ask them about it, they will tell their story ... period. Regarding the experiencers, "Their life has gained in depth.... In no case have they taken on the idea of instant salvation or moral infallibility," says van Lommel.

The miraculously healed may be officially recognized or not, but all experience a miraculous healing that cannot be medically explained; they attest to a complete change of perspective on life. All of them claim to have experienced a *before* and *after* much like NDE experiencers have. Their lives are transformed on all levels.[18] For both groups, it is about a unique personal experience that requires decryption and authentication to assure reliability regarding both reason and faith.

Finally, neither NDEs nor miracles can be explained by physiological, psychological, cultural, or religious causes. They are medically inexplicable. In fact, there are no "scientific" proofs for their existence, since modern scientific methods are not adapted to evaluate such human experiences. Instead, we have many "signs," some more specific than others, that leave us to decide for ourselves whether we believe in them or not.

There is also the fact that some NDEs can incite physical or psychological healing, something that, I must admit, does not surprise me.

Among the many testimonies he receives from around the world, Jeffrey Long says that as a physician, he is fascinated with the numerous stories about unexpected healings. The words *miracle* and *healing* are repeated dozens of times. He cannot guarantee that these recoveries happen because of NDEs but he does suspect this nonetheless. He further wishes to devote some of his research on the study of these miraculous healings.

Dr. Sylvie Déthiollaz, biologist and founder of the Noesis Center, has offered several examples.[19] Certain people with terminal cancer have healed rapidly without any apparent medical explanation, as if the submersion in light—as experienced during the NDE—had given the person the strength to heal. That is it! Dr. Déthiollaz does not claim it, but I do believe that, in such cases, we could speak of miracles. I will explain in greater detail.

Others have experienced this healing much like an accelerated psychoanalysis, in which the person has access to information—in general, during the life review—that will allow him to understand the origins of an ancient trauma that was deeply buried until then, and to find a way out of this trauma.[20] Here also, if we have faith that God intervenes on our behalf to enlighten us, I do not see why we cannot speak of a miracle, even if the healing is only of a psychological nature. In fact, first and foremost there is a healing of love of self. It is an instantaneous therapy that allows the experiencer to accept himself as he is and without condition. As one experiencer said, "God loves me simply as I am." Personally, I am not surprised by this.

Let us consider the fact that there is no medical explanation for a miraculous healing, and that it presents with characteristics that are unknown to modern medicine, including a spontaneous remission without need for convalescence and resulting in perfect health. Once we consider all of this, there is no way we are not drawn to understand what might be happening here. The healed are average down-to-earth people. There must be an internal mechanism that is swift—even instantaneous—in its effect on the body. Where might this come from? It is impossible that it comes from the body, which, as we know, does not have the capacity to have such an effect on itself. Nor can the psyche have such an effect. The placebo effect or the Coué method can be invoked here, but if either of these were the case, why then does it not happen more often, especially under the supervision of psychologists or psychiatrists?

The origins of these healings are surely of a different order. Indeed, they most often happen in a faith-oriented context. This is especially evident within the vicinity of the Lourdes Sanctuary. Still, some of them happen elsewhere (for instance, on the way to or from the sanctuary, or anywhere even). Furthermore, some people were able to heal at Lourdes without even knowing what this sanctuary represents or without any connection to the faith or being from a different religion. (I note many healings of Muslim women.) Many of the healed never expected the healing would happen, even moments before the event. "Belief" in the healing is therefore not a good explanation for its occurrence. It can then be said that a miraculous healing is not dependent on the person being healed. Nonetheless, there is indeed a healing process happening in this person. If it does not come from the body nor from the psyche, its origin can only be from within the spiritual soul. This is, indeed, what I have always believed. Jean-Pierre Bély is the miraculously healed person that I have studied the most and that I know best. He always said to those who would listen that he had been touched by a spiritual force once unknown to him by receiving three healing sacraments from the church: reconciliation, Eucharist, and anointing of the sick. He added that the energy he received had broadcast and deployed itself throughout his body and to each of his cells, healing him completely. Like all of the miraculously healed, he was immediately aware of this instantaneous healing and was immediately liberated from the pain he suffered for over sixteen years. He had suffered from severe multiple sclerosis, and the Social Security Department had declared him 100 percent disabled with lifelong dependence on a third party. After he returned home, he was riding his bicycle!

It therefore has to be from the deepest and most sacred part of our being, the spiritual heart, that this process unfolds. This spiritual heart is innate in everyone—believers and nonbelievers alike. Similarly for

NDEs, the person goes through a holy encounter—an "extreme" and otherworldly encounter. It should not be surprising to note that the experiencer can be healed of previous ills.

Jeffrey Long offers some examples of people who are blind from birth and who were able to see during their NDE; they have a kind of "visual" experience because they do not know what it is to really see.[21] This produces an event that is medically inexplicable, says Long. He continues that, nonetheless, *they can instantly see as soon as their NDE begins, and they have a detailed and organized visual experience.* This event can only be understood if we infer that blind experiencers have been in contact with a God who does not want them to remain blind. In heaven, there will not be any blind people or lame people!

Jeffrey Long also recognizes that *vision described during NDEs is different from earthly vision, which is so familiar to us…. It is more vivid, comprehensive, and nonphysical,* which is correct in the case of miracles.

In Lourdes, blind people have had vision. Their sight originated not in the physical body but truly from a "celestial" place. Miraculous healings have therefore implicated the same kind of intervention that finds its origins in the effusion of the Holy Spirit in us—in our spiritual soul—radiating throughout the body. Its occurrence does not depend on us; it depends on God alone.

The Almighty has all the power to heal; that is, if he finds reason to use his power! Some have recovered their sight after an NDE while others have not. We are not the ones who know what is best for us and for our ultimate destiny!

> After this, I saw a large crowd with more people than could be counted. They were from every race, tribe, nation, and language, and they stood before the throne and before the Lamb. They wore white robes and held palm branches in their hands (Revelation 7:9).

—◦◦◦—

"A Priest Who Saw Hell, Purgatory, and Heaven"

I am the eldest of seven children. I was born on July 16, 1949, in Kerala, India.

At the age of fourteen, I entered St. Mary's Minor Seminary in Thiruvalla to begin my studies for the priesthood. Four years later I went to St. Joseph's Pontifical Major Seminary in Alwaye, Kerala, to continue my priestly formation. After completing the seven years of philosophy and theology, I was ordained a priest on January 1, 1975, to serve as a missionary at the Diocese of Thiruvalla.

On Sunday, April 14, 1985, the Feast of the Divine Mercy, I was going to celebrate Mass at a mission church in the northern part of Kerala, and I had a fatal accident. I was riding a motorcycle when I was hit head-on by a jeep driven by a man who was intoxicated after a Hindu festival. I was rushed to a hospital about thirty-five miles away. On the way my soul came out of my body and I experienced death. Immediately I met my guardian angel. I saw my body and the people who were carrying me to the hospital. I heard them crying and praying for me. At this time my angel told me: "I am going to take you to heaven. The Lord wants to meet you and talk with you." He also said that on the way he wanted to show me hell and purgatory.

First, the angel escorted me to hell. It was an awful sight! I saw Satan and the devils, an unquenchable fire of about two thousand degrees Fahrenheit, worms crawling, people screaming and fighting, others being tortured by demons. The angel told me that all these sufferings were due to unrepented mortal sins. Then I understood that there are seven degrees, or levels, of suffering according to the number and kinds of mortal sins committed in their earthly lives. The souls looked very ugly, cruel and horrific. It was a fearful experience. I saw people I knew but I am not allowed to reveal their identities. The sins that convicted them were mainly abortion, homosexuality, euthanasia, hatefulness, unforgiveness, and sacrilege. The angel told me that if they had repented they would have avoided hell and gone instead to purgatory. I also understood that some people who repent from these sins might be purified on earth through their sufferings. This way they can avoid purgatory and go straight to heaven.

I was surprised when I saw in hell even priests and bishops, some of whom I never expected to see. Many of them were there because they had misled people with false teaching and bad example.

After the visit to hell, my guardian angel escorted me to purgatory. Here too there are seven degrees of suffering and unquenchable fire. But it is far less intense than hell and there was neither quarreling nor fighting. The main suffering of these souls is their separation from God. Some of those who are in purgatory committed numerous mortal sins but they were reconciled with God before their death. Even though these souls are suffering, they enjoy peace and the knowledge that one day they will see God face to face.

I had a chance to communicate with the souls in purgatory. They asked me to pray for them and to tell the people to pray for them as well, so they can go to heaven quickly. When we pray for these souls we will receive their gratitude through their prayers and once they enter heaven their prayers become even more meritorious.

It is difficult for me to describe how beautiful my guardian angel is. He is radiant and bright. He is my constant companion and helps me in all my ministries, especially my healing ministry. I experience his presence everywhere I go and I am grateful for his protection in my daily life.

Next, my angel escorted me to heaven, passing through a big, dazzling-white tunnel. I never experienced this much peace and joy in my life. Then immediately heaven opened up and I heard the most delightful music, which I had never heard before. The angels were singing and praising God. I saw all the saints, especially the Blessed Mother and Saint Joseph, and many dedicated holy bishops and priests who were shining like stars. And when I appeared before the Lord, Jesus told me, "I want you to go back to the world. In your second life you will be an instrument of peace and healing to my people. You will walk in a foreign land and you will speak in a foreign tongue. Everything is possible for you with my grace." After these words, the Blessed Mother told me, "Do whatever he tells you. I will help you in your ministries."

Words cannot express the beauty of heaven. There we find so much peace and happiness, which exceed a million times our imagination. Our Lord is far more beautiful than any image can convey. His face is radiant and luminous and more beautiful than a thousand rising suns. The pictures we see in the world are only a shadow of his magnificence. The Blessed Mother was next to Jesus; she was so beautiful and radiant. None of the images we see in this world can compare with her real beauty. Heaven is our real home. We are all created to reach heaven and enjoy God forever. Then, I came back to the world with my angel.

While my body was at the hospital, the doctor completed all examinations and I was pronounced dead. The cause of death was bleeding. My family was notified and since they were far away, the hospital staff decided to move my dead body to the morgue. Because the hospital did not have air conditioners they were concerned that the body would decompose quickly. As they were moving my dead body to the morgue, my soul came back to the body. I felt an excruciating pain because I had so many wounds and broken bones. I began to scream and then the people became frightened and ran away screaming. One of them approached the doctor and said, "The dead body is screaming." The doctor came to examine the body and found that I was alive. So he said, "Father is alive; it is a miracle. Take him back to the hospital."

Back at the hospital they gave me blood transfusions and I was taken to surgery to repair the broken bones. They worked on my lower jaw, ribs, pelvic bone, wrists, and right leg. After two months, I was released from the hospital, but my orthopedic doctor said that I would never walk again. I then said to him, "The Lord who gave me my life back and sent me back to the world will heal me." Once at home we were all praying for a miracle. Still after a month and with the casts removed I was not able to move. But one day while praying I felt an extraordinary pain in my pelvic area. After a short while, the pain disappeared completely and I heard a voice saying, "You are healed. Get up and walk." I felt the peace and healing power on my body. I immediately got up and walked. I praised and thanked God for the miracle.

I reached my doctor with the news of my healing and he was amazed. He said, "Your God is the true God. I must follow your God." The doctor was Hindu and he asked me to teach him about our church. After studying the faith, I baptized him and he became Catholic.

Following the message from my guardian angel, I came to the United States on November 10, 1986, as a missionary priest.... From June 1999 to June 2011, I was pastor of St. Mary, Mother of Mercy Catholic Church in Macclenny, Florida.[1]

—Father Jose Maniyangat

Two Homilies—Meditations

Easter Sunday—A Breach in Our Earth

Acts 10:34, 37–43; Psalm 117; Colossians 3:1 –4; John 20:1–9

In those days, all was as usual: speech was at its most powerful, the law did not protect the feeblest ones, and men of heart were subjected to humiliating deaths.

In those days, claiming that *the souls of the righteous are in the hand of God* made no sense whatsoever.... Jesus himself suffered these doubts— he who pronounced these words from the cross: *My God, my God, why have you forsaken me?* His terrible plea would culminate in the hope of resurrection, as is stated in the Psalms,[2] but the hope cannot erase the terror of doubt embedded in his plea....

In those days, Jesus was entombed and all was over: the stone sealed the entrance, which was cavalierly guarded....

Still, that morning, when night was just starting to give way to daylight, after all the excitement of the last few days, Mary Magdalene goes to visit the tomb.

On that day, nothing is as usual. Everything seems to tumble just like the stone tumbled to allow life to have free rein....

On that day, it is finished: The Father proclaims to the world that *the souls of the righteous are in the hand of God* and that the earth would not hold back the One who entrusted his life to God. The first witnesses—Mary Magdalene, Peter, and John—notice that the stone had been moved and the sepulcher was empty.

Brothers and sisters, the sepulcher is no longer the end of our lives; it has become a "passage." The Son of God showed us the way through the great mystery of his passage....

On that day, in a giddy moment of intuition like no other in a man's life—a brainwave like a stupendous lightning strike—John hears the resonating sound of Jesus's words. He makes sense of them as he is standing in front of the empty sepulcher and he suddenly understands the meaning of the human adventure: "He saw, and believed." He himself proclaims it in a brief moment of certainty, if any there was! Nothing will be as before: the Good News is born....

Our God continues to surprise us. Contemplating human life and existence, we are drawn to give him thanks for everything. But our God, Father of Jesus Christ, is better yet. Through Jesus, he gives us hope in a new life. When our life force diminishes and the breath of life abandons us, God himself gathers us and welcomes us. Thus, life as we currently know it suddenly appears to be just a first step. In Jesus Christ we discover that *we were created to live, live again, always live.*

Death is indeed a fact that cannot be eliminated, but it is no longer the same! A long time ago, the sea opened up to create a "passage" toward liberty. A nation was born. Today, the open earth becomes the "passage" from death to life. A hope is born....

Dear Christians, our life is no easier than that of others. We are subjected to the same challenges, but a certainty guides us: nothing will be lost of what we devote ourselves to and what we go through. All of this is our way of building ourselves a new life. Our passage through the tomb—this mysterious crucible—will make of us this man, this woman, who will go forth in God's glory beyond the breach. This certainty leads the way to a profound sense of joy and hope that can enlighten our life....

On this Easter Sunday, just as the open sepulcher confirmed the resurrection of Jesus, may the Lord grant us his Spirit by way of the broken bread, and may he *make us living beings from now into the life he has promised us in the eternal Easter....*

Christ is resurrected, he is really resurrected! Amen! Hallelujah!

———

Commemoration of All the Faithful Departed

Book of Wisdom 2:23, 3:1–6, 9; Psalms 4:2, 7, 9;
Romans 6:3 –9; John 4:1 –6

Where are they and what has become of them, our grandparents, our parents, our husbands and wives, our brothers, our sisters, our children, our friends and acquaintances who are deceased and who we once accompanied to a church, a funeral, or a cemetery? Where are they and what has become of them? Some people say that they simply disappeared, and that is possibly true … because something irreversible has occurred. We can no longer see them. They are no longer talking to us. They no longer participate in our activities. O death, "irreparable loss!"[3] In pain and in loss, in regret and in weakness, we also think of death in this way. But then, what can this celebration of the second of November—this day of commemoration for the deceased—bring us? Are we gathered here to remember the emotional shock of mourning? No!

Two scriptures have just penetrated our ears. They can change our perspective on death. The first scripture comes from the first letter excerpted from the Book of Wisdom: *And their going forth from us, seemed utter destruction. But they are in peace.* The second scripture comes from the Gospel: *The hour is coming … when the dead shall hear the voice of the Son of God, and they that hear shall live.* These two scriptures should not be considered anesthesia against the pain of death. They don't bring about a kind of pious comforting. Instead, they help us realize that our death does not in fact mean complete annihilation. So how is this possible? What should we believe, especially since we recognize resurrection of the dead and eternal life as phenomena? What should we believe? What should we think? This is especially true considering that *the essential question that confronts life is the notion of death.*[4] Our faith in God must be able to respond to this question. And what does our faith have to say?

Before answering this question, let's look more closely into the human experience.[5] Man essentially fears two things: solitude and nonsurvival. When facing the fear of solitude, man finds a solution that consists in opening himself up to another in friendship, in marriage, or whatever can help him not be alone. Unfortunately, when we look at it concretely, we might quickly realize that this solution is limited. No one can reach intimately into another person's heart to fill a void. All coupled or group life, all encounters—no matter how beautiful—can only diminish solitude for a short time. We eventually are left alone to examine our own anxieties. When facing the second existential fear—which is due to the fact that man cannot be invincible to time—a person may try two different solutions. First, he may try to find survival or a certain immortality in his own children. But here again, he quickly realizes that finding survival in one's own children is not realistic. Then, he tries to survive on his own potential. He takes refuge in the notion that he might find glory in being remembered by others after his passing. There again, he fails, because after his death, man realizes that what will be left of his glory, what will remain, is not himself but a simple echo or a mere shadow of himself. Worse, the one who was to remember him will also return to dust. This is a double failure of this endeavor toward survival.

God is there to rescue man under these circumstances of failure. Our faith affirms that at a certain point, God made himself flesh. Moreover, he crossed the threshold of death and came out victorious. He descended in the depths of our solitude. Where no other man could enter, Jesus took a seat there. Where no word could reach us, he made himself Word and entered our hearts. That which might have seemed inconsolable in a man, Jesus saw it and empathized. The "descent into hell," as it is taught in our credo, means just this. The solitude of death was frequented by Jesus. Furthermore, Jesus himself, who passed from death into life, can undertake the responsibility for our survival. Our name can stay with him and thereby transcend time. Those whose names survive the test of time are called saints. The celebration of All Saints Day reminds us of this. The saints are our dead; they are our dead that do not die in our thoughts because they live in God's thought. How can this be possible? Well, all this was made possible because of the GREAT LOVE that God granted us in his Son, Jesus. Yes, love generates immortality. Let's remember how difficult it is for us to forget those who we loved or who made us feel good. Let's also recall that it's love that assures the survival of the species. Spiritually speaking, it's also through love, the gift of himself, and the gift of his life that Christ awakens the human species from death because humans cannot make life last forever. Thus, when we say that "love is greater than death," we are not speaking in simple terms; instead, we are talking about a truth that makes perfect sense in relation to Christ.

Love is also a means of understanding all of the discourses on the afterlife, including the "famous" hell, the Resurrection, paradise, and eternal life. In fact, hell does not consist in a physical fire or a place of torture that was prepared by God to punish us.[6] Hell is the state of solitude that refuses God's love. Resurrection and eternal life represent the state in which God's love breaks the solitude of death and becomes our way of life. It all begins with baptism, this beautiful sacrament of love and connection between God and the human soul. Once baptized, our life is connected with God, and death cannot cause a relapse into solitude if we remain connected to him. To do this, we must renew our life, we must not be afraid to begin again, we must not give up the fight in order to pick ourselves up and try again, with our eyes focused on the Lord who is forever calling our attention. Finally, our relationship to the deceased can only be understood through love as well. Even if we need to strike out their name and address from our address books, even if we need to stow away their clothing and close their apartments, these last vestiges that exclude them from our daily lives bring us to look for them and find them at God's side through "our" prayer and the Mass, "Jesus's saving grace."[7] These two actions unite us in God and to those who live for him. Then this November 2 is a time of loving communion and of dialogue with our deceased loved ones. Let us remember them more than ever and let us be carried by God's love, which has the power to unite us all in him.

Lord, grant our deceased loved ones eternal rest; may the everlasting Light shine bright in their eyes—the Light that entered their life the day of their baptism, the day of the beginning of their life in You and with You.

—Abbott Innocent Essonam Padanassirou

Conclusion

This death which seems, as seen from this side,
Like a dive into the shadow,
Is a splendid entrance into the light of God.
  —Pierre Sertillanges

It is possible to not believe in life after death. Medical science believes that the brain's death is the end of life. Nonetheless, something out of the ordinary happens at the moment of death, whether it is a brutal death or not. All testimonies of those who have experienced a near-death experience suggest that this is not a journey to the end of life. Quite the contrary, it is an opening into a kind of gateway intersecting two worlds: our own world, the one we have always known—which has satisfied our basic needs until now and of which we have a hard time letting go—and another world, which is paradoxically compelling to those who claim they have experienced it. This other world recaps our whole existence in a beautifully enlightening way such that we are projected into the clarity of a whole other, hard-to-imagine universe. It is like a new beginning.

Near-death experiences therefore call on us to believe in a personal existence that transcends clinical death; this resonates with the Christian belief that affirms the continuation of our personal life beyond death. More astonishing yet, many experiencers relate their experience of being in the presence of complete love, in a place of desolation, or in a place of purification, concepts that correspond to the typically Christian notions of heaven, hell, and purgatory.

Of course, I am not advocating that we fall prey to gullibility. We must keep a critical eye on everything, both in terms of reason as well as faith. Still, all testimonies and current scientific studies concur: *near-death experiences are as authentic as any other human perception; they are as indubitable as math and as real as language,* says Dr. Melvin Morse.[1]

From a religious perspective, we have been able to subject these testimonies to the Word of God through various passages from the scriptures, as well as to Christian anthropology, miraculous healing experiences, apparitions, and even surprising mystical experiences that have existed throughout Christian history: there is no contradiction. We can further rely on Saint Thomas Aquinas, the angelic doctor, through an article by Howard Kainz:

> In the *Summa Theologiae*, he probes Scripture, Aristotle, the writings of Augustine and other Fathers, and offers some conclusions that seem to dovetail with NDE literature. For example, he says the soul freed from the body will be in one sense incomplete, since it has a natural orientation towards union with the body, but it will also have "greater freedom of intelligence, since the weight and care of the body is a clog upon the clearness of its intelligence in the present life."
>
> Thus Aquinas agrees with the unanimous testimony of NDERs about the tremendous freedom and intellectual clarity that characterized the separation [of body and soul]. Also, the separated soul will not be able to have any influence on material things. This echoes the experience of NDERs who experience themselves going through walls and other material things....
>
> Finally, there will be no faith, since faith is of things unseen, nor hope, since hope is of things not yet possessed, but only charity, which remains in the next life, and even will be the measure of an individual's happiness: "The greater the charity from which our actions proceed, the more perfectly shall we enjoy God."
>
> It is possible that NDEs give us an indication of what the initial entrance into the afterlife is like. But since nothing impure can enter into the presence of God, most of us may need to slowly learn to leave behind a lot of bad habits we hold quite dear.[2]

Thus, if NDEs approach the traditional teachings of the Catholic Church, *we can admit that there is life after death without even needing to be a believer or believing in the resurrection of Christ.* As long as we have tried to avoid wrongdoing and to truly love, our death will not be an impasse or a descent into a complete void. Instead, it will be an irruption into an eternal bliss in the presence of God of Mercy, in a perfect union with the Creator himself, versus an idyllic world that could provide us everything we missed in this world:[3] Heaven awaits "those who die in God's grace and friendship and are perfectly purified live forever with Christ. They are like God forever for they 'see him as he is' [1 John 3:2], face-to-face."[4] In fact, "by his death and resurrection, Jesus Christ has "opened" heaven to us"[5] and has annihilated death for us. His resurrection is a guarantee of our own resurrection. We will live forever. *Life is greater than death.* Death is a passage, a step. Another life awaits us, this one more beautiful, richer, and more marvelous.

Of course, if we must pass through death, which is unfortunately a separation, a rupture of human love, NDEs also bring us the shocking revelation that we will rejoin those who we loved in this life, those who we loved *in God*; if we truly love, then we will never lose any of those we have so loved. It is Christ's promise: *love is greater than death*; so in another life, in the afterlife, we will rejoin those we loved, which is exactly like the Catholic tenet of the communion of saints.

Thus, in this new millennium, if we have *a confirmation of what Christianity has always taught us*, why would we reject it? Due to the strength and specificity of the Christian faith, the church indeed offers freely all that we need to lead a life that points the way to eternal bliss: through the Sacraments, the sanctification of time (through liturgy), prayer, the right and voluntary actions that help us realize the double commandment of charity (love God and your neighbor as yourself).

Our society, which proclaims its expertise for so many things in so many areas—up to the point of manipulating human life itself—finds its limitations in death as if it were an absurdity. We are to the point of promoting *the death of death* thanks to nanotechnology, biotechnology, information technology, and cognitive science (the NBIC technologies), and artificial intelligence (AI) of transhumanism: "Yesterday's science fiction wants to be today's medicine!"[6] Otherwise, there is a sense that we can control the time of death: Are euthanasia and assisted suicide not ways to evade death by provoking it? Should we not refuse that some want to *rob us of our death*, this period of time that is so important, precious, and unique, where our life is recapped before its passage into another life?

The Christian faith considers the time of death as fundamental—a time to live, to live as well as possible by preparing oneself for death and by praying in request for "the grace of a good death." We have good reason to invoke the Virgin Mary every day to accompany us "now and at the hour of our death," these two most important moments of our lives! Yes, God, Christ, the Virgin Mary, the angels, and the saints in heaven[7] will rush to our bedside in the moments immediately preceding our death. The devil as well will come seeking to torment us, wanting for us to miss *this meeting of all-consuming love*, requiring that we give ourselves fully to this process with complete detachment, abandon, confidence, and charity.[8]

In fact, this brings us to inquire about life: We are so attached to this life—with good reason. Can we actually understand it all?

It is indeed perfectly invisible, always mysterious.

Let us note that our instinct to live and to survive is the primary impetus of the whole of living beings—as much in the crudest of species as in the most elaborate ones, and as much in the deepest abyss as on the surface of the earth; everything is oriented toward the transmission of life. Throughout the universe, life seems to hold primary importance, seems to be an absolute.

However, life is a concept that paradoxically has escaped the stronghold of science, which has yet to clearly define what life is. Life in itself cannot be found under the scalpel or under the microscope. There is no trace of life; there is no vestige of life. Life reveals itself only in living beings. The human being studies himself, which is the object of biology, but life does not observe itself. Life experiences itself (especially in the present, *in the present moment*).

In order to have life on earth, we must admit that there is one chance in billions and billions, which is semi-impossible. It necessitates a true miracle.

This life, through which a person can be assured of his continuance for all of existence, has not been acquired through our own efforts or by our merits! It does not come from us; we do not give it to ourselves. *Life is a gift that we receive freely.* Someone gave it to us. Obviously, our parents transferred it to us, but *the source of all life can only be in God,* Creator and Father of both the visible and invisible universe.

Frankly then, if God—who is absolute love—gives life, how could we imagine that he would want to take it back from us? No, he gives it and gives it again. It is like this for eternity!

These NDEs can only be received in the same way. We cannot make them happen by willing them. They are signs of life from beyond, and they open us up to an invisible reality. Maybe it would be best to call them "Openings on Invisible Life" (OIL). I am convinced that these openings are a *sign of the times.* They are calling on all of us at the beginning of this millennium that we may not be swayed by doubt. They have a lot to teach us about our human nature and our destiny. Moreover, in this world of disbelief, withdrawal, and isolation, as if God did not exist, I believe NDEs are *signs of heaven* that are meant to awaken our interest in invisible things. These are times when Western man has chased out of heaven all the beings he thought he had seen there, and where death is being censured as an unwholesome occurrence. Paradoxically, through new channels in line with our times, heaven is repopulating itself! God still has something to teach; why then would he not give us a sign in this way?

Near-death experiences help us understand that we are passers-by and pilgrims on this earth, preparing for a new reality. In each moment, we get to choose between life and death. If we decidedly choose life, we will from then on submerse ourselves without fear in the great ocean of love of divine mercy.

> But if Christ is in you, though the body is dead because of sin, the Spirit is life because of righteousness. If the Spirit of him who raised Jesus from the dead dwells in you, he who raised Christ from the dead will give life to your mortal bodies also through his Spirit that dwells in you (Romans 8:10–11).

—◦◦◦—

Epilogue

A Slit Throat

This story associates near-death experiences and healing in an exceptional way. It could be ancient, dating from 1858, but it is incontestably verifiable by the cross-checking it has been subjected to. We are talking about Mariam Baouardy, who was born in 1846 in Palestine, Galilea, from a poor but pious family of the Melkite Greek Catholic faith. At age twenty, she entered the Carmel of Pau,[1] where she took the name of Sister Mary of Jesus Crucified, though she was called the Little Arab. She was very humble (even calling herself "the little nothing"), and she remained "lay sister" her whole life because of ignorance and her inability to read, write, study, or to sing the Mass.

Mariam was practical and grounded. She was a rugged initiator, responsible for the establishment of the Carmel of Mangalore in India and then the Carmel of Bethlehem, where she died at the age of thirty-three (August 28, 1878) following an accident.

As we can see, she was not an "enlightened one," but she benefited from a great number of extraordinary mystical experiences throughout her life,[2] many of which have been carefully studied.

There is abundant credible documentation on her life from accessible sources. For instance, a biography was written by many authors including Father Pierre Estrate, her spiritual father, who was charged by then Bishop Lacroix with writing everything he knew about her. There can therefore be no doubt about the events she experienced. I drew her story from the excellent book by Friar Amédée Brunot, who offers all necessary references.[3]

Orphaned at the age of three, her adoptive parents leave Galilea to establish themselves in Alexandria, Egypt. Following the customs of the time, her parents attempt to wed her with an uncle without consulting her. Mariam categorically refuses. Furious, the uncle treats her like a slave for three months. Neither one is willing to yield. Wanting to rejoin her little brother who was left behind in Galilea, she escapes one night and reconnects with an old servant of the family, a Muslim who is about to leave for Nazareth. He tries to make her abandon her Catholic faith to become a Muslim. The girl's fiery temperament resists the man's proposal with fervor. Furious from being put in his place by this little Christian girl, the man reacts violently, unsheathes his scimitar and slits the girl's throat. He wraps her in a large shroud and, assisted by his mother and his wife, he leaves her bloody body in a dark alley.

This drama unfolds on the night of September 7 to September 8, 1858.

Here is how Friar Brunot recounts Mariam's tale:

Later, when she was forced to tell her story and to relate the details of her martyrdom, Mariam declared that she was truly dead. In Marseille, the teacher of novices asked her if she had been subjected to the final judgment. She replied,

"No, but I found myself in heaven with the Blessed Virgin, the angels and the saints. They treated me with great kindness. In their company were my parents. I saw the brilliant throne of the Most Holy Trinity and Jesus Christ in His humanity. There was no sun, no lamp, but everything was bright with light. Someone spoke to me. They said, 'You are truly a virgin, but your book is unfinished.'"[4]

That is it for her NDE. The following details deserve to be told. Once her vision was done, Mariam found herself in a grotto. Standing next to her was a nun dressed in blue who told her she picked her up in the alley. The nun brought Mariam to the grotto and stitched her neck wound. This mysterious sister of charity with a blue habit was of great sensitivity. She spoke very little, spending most of her time taking care of the girl by wetting her lips with cotton, letting her sleep, and giving her soup to bring her back to strength. She looked like no other sister.

Once the wound had scarred over, the nun brought Mariam out of the grotto. She took her to the Church of Saint-Catherine, which was served by the Franciscan Friars; and there, she called on a confessor.

When Mariam exited the confessional, she was alone. The nurse with a blue habit had disappeared!

Who was she? In 1874, on the anniversary of the attack and the feast of our Lady's nativity, Mariam proclaimed in ecstasy, *On this same day in 1858, I was with my Mother and I consecrated my life to her. Someone had cut my throat and the next day Mother Mary took care of me.*

Once again, in August 1875, when she was on a boat going toward Palestine, she recounted what she remembered to her director, Father Estrate, and she stated precisely, *I know now that the religious who cared for me after my martyrdom was the Blessed Virgin.* During her trip from Alexandria with a group of Carmelites, on their way to found the Carmel of Bethlehem, Mariam directed the caravan to go visit the Church of Saint-Catherine and the grotto, transformed into halls by the Greek Catholics.

Friar Brunot asked an essential question:

How can we be assured that these marvelous situations really happened? Certainly, we only have Mariam's testimony to go by. The murderer never made himself known. The nun who took care of the child also never revealed her identity. We can guess why! As for the orphan's parents, they knew nothing about the details of the tragedy; they thought that Mariam had escaped to resist her mistreatment and that she had possibly gotten lost in the mayhem of the city of Alexandria. They had every interest in keeping the silence on the unfortunate circumstances of their adoptee! She would otherwise be a dishonor to the family.

We are therefore left with Mariam's testimony to rely on. It is upheld by the seriousness, sincerity, and humility with which she led her life, as witnesses have corroborated. Many details were later attested to by her brother, Boulos: he indeed received the famous letter from his sister. He answered the call by traveling to Alexandria, but since his sister was no longer at the uncle's house, he returned to Galilea. There is one irrefutable fact: she had a scar on her neck. Many physicians and nurses noticed the scar during many illnesses Mariam suffered, either in Marseille, in Pau, in Mangalore, or in Bethlehem. The scar measured four inches long and about three-eighths of an inch wide; it spanned the front of the neck. The skin was thinner and whiter there. Several of the rings of the trachea were missing, as the physician of Pau noticed on June 24, 1875. The teacher of novices wrote, "A famous doctor from Marseille who was an atheist had treated Mariam and afterward admitted that there must be a God, otherwise, she would not have survived." Following this deep wound, Mariam had a broken voice.

Friar Brunot concluded: *The martyrdom of the little Arab was not a fantasy. It remained inscribed in her flesh.*

Mariam's exceptionally pure heart led her to see the celestial truths (the Virgin showed her heaven, hell, and the purgatory!), which in turn allowed her to bear witness to them by her whole life.

She was beatified by John Paul II in 1983 and canonized on May 17, 2015, by Pope Francis.

A Prayer

In the Saint-Jacques de Pau Church during Holy Week at the twelfth station of the cross.

Lord, as people who are well fed, well housed, comfortably settled, our illness is that we fear death. You who are dead and who will resurrect, teach us to love death. It is our second cradle. Grant us firm footing as we walk toward it. It promises us a perfect life. And then, teach us to have an insatiable curiosity for the afterlife: "Up there, everything will be love." Let us savor this perfume of love that will lead to paradise with each step, each gesture, each beat of the heart. We will then live in joy.

Notes

Introduction

1. See Terry K. Basford, *Near-Death Experiences* (Garland Publishing: New York, 1990), which inventoried over seven hundred references on this subject, most of which were from scientific sources.
2. In 1993, only 8 percent of the French still believed in resurrection. Where are we today?
3. I prefer not to report on Eastern religions; others have done so in the references I have listed.

What Is a Near-Death Experience?

1. Raymond Moody, *Life after Life* (Marietta, GA: Mockingbird Books, 1975), 21–22.
2. Evelyn Elsaesser-Valarino, "Dialogue with Kenneth Ring," in *On the Other Side of Life: Exploring the Phenomenon of Near-Death Experience* (New York: Da Capo Press, 1997). In the entire world, this number would be in the order of sixty million.
3. Using a statistic of three hundred million people in the United States compared with sixty million in France; that is, five times less.
4. www.nderf.org.
5. Jeffrey Long and Paul Perry, *Evidence of the Afterlife: The Science of Near-Death Experiences* (New York: HarperCollins, 2010), 2.
6. Some have noted twelve or fifteen.
7. Reedited in pocket format in 2012.
8. Furthermore, her allegiance to the Mormon faith has surely imparted in her certain beliefs, such as a prenatal existence, which, for me, does not take away from the rest.
9. Betty J. Eadie, "My Death," chapter 4, in *Embraced by the Light* (Warren, MI: Gold Leaf Press, 1992).
10. Long and Perry, *Evidence of the Afterlife*.
11. Eadie, "My Death," chapter 4, in *Embraced by the Light*.
12. Ibid.
13. Betty J. Eadie, "The Tunnel," chapter 5, in *Embraced by the Light*.
14. Ibid.
15. Margot Grey, *Return from Death: An Exploration of Near-Death Experience* (Boston: Arkana, 1985), 50.

16. He recounts his story of NDE in George Ritchie, *Return from Tomorrow* (Ada, MI: Chosen Books, 2007).

17. "Heaven and Hell: Dr. George Ritchie's Near-Death Experience," http://bibleprobe.com/drrichie.htm.

18. Moody, *Life after Life*, 56.

19. Ibid.

20. Raymond Moody, *The Light Beyond* (New York: Bantam, 1989).

21. Betty J. Eadie, "In the Arms of Light," chapter 6, in *Embraced by the Light*.

22. Ibid.

23. Moody, *Life after Life*.

24. Kenneth Ring, *Heading Toward Omega: In Search of the Meaning of the Near-Death Experience* (New York: William Morrow, 1984).

25. Kenneth Ring, "Amazing Grace: The NDE as a Compensatory Gift," *Journal of Near-Death Studies* 10, no. 1 (1991): 11–29.

26. Grey, *Return from Death*.

27. Betty J. Eadie, "My Return," chapter 18, in *Embraced by the Light*.

28. Ibid.

29. Betty J. Eadie, "My Recovery," chapter 19, in *Embraced by the Light*.

30. I concluded this with a number of people who were healed—whether they were recognized as miraculously healed or not—by interviewing them or their next of kin. I transcribed a maximum of these experiences in my latest book, *Lourdes : des miracles pour notre guérison* [Lourdes: miracles for our healing] (Paris: Presses de la Renaissance, 2008).

31. Moody, *Life after Life*.

32. Kenneth Ring and Evelyn Elsaesser-Valarino, *Lessons from the Light: What We Can Learn from the Near-Death Experience* (Needham, MA: Moment Point Press, 2006).

33. Ring, *Heading Toward Omega*.

34. A general estimate of about 2 to 3 percent has been proposed; the Near Death Experience Research Foundation (NERF) reported 7 of 161 cases were frightening experiences, based on data collection over five months.

35. Maurice Rawlings, *Beyond Death's Door* (New York: Bantam, 1991).

36. A palliative care nurse in the United Kingdom and a leading expert in the field of NDEs, Sartori presented a paper on the topic at the Second International Medical Conference on Near-Death Experiences, Conference Proceedings, Marseille, France, March 9–10, 2013. S17 Production.

37. Institut Suisse de Sciences Noétiques (ISSNOE) [Swiss Institute of Noetic Sciences], www.issnoe.ch.

Second Testimony

1. Patrick Drouot, *Nous sommes tous immortels* [We are all immortals] (Monaco: Editions du Rocher, 1997).

Historical Comparisons

1. Gregory of Tours, *Historia Francorum*, vol. 7, chap. 1.
2. Michel Aupetit, *La mort, et après ?* [Death, and then?] (Paris: Salvator, 2009).
3. The painting, a panel from an altarpiece thought to be of the Last Judgement (oil on panel), is exhibited at Palazzo Ducale, Doge's Palace, Venice, Italy.
4. Moody used the same expression—"near-death experience"—that French psychologist and epistemologist Victor Egger proposed in 1896 in *The Self of the Dying,* following debates between psychologists and philosophers about the Albert Heim stories in the Swiss Alpine Club annals.
5. See his book *La source noire : Révélations aux portes de la mort* [The black source: revelations at the edge of death] (Paris: Livre de Poche, 1987).
6. Dr. Moody has always made a point to emphasize that he never belonged to the New Age movement.
7. Sonia Barkallah produced another film, *Faux départ : Enquête sur les experiences de mort imminente* [False start: inquiry into near-death experiences], in 2010 (www.S17productions.com).
8. The Weighted Score Experience Index (WCEI) was created in 1980 by the psychologist Kenneth Ring, and the Near-Death Experience Scale was developed by Bruce Greyson in 1983 to measure the depth of an individual's near-death experience.
9. Miracles also rely on testimonies!
10. Just as there is no humanly acceptable response to the fact that some people are miraculously healed while others are not.
11. Second International Medical Conference on Near-Death Experiences, Conference Proceedings, S17 Production, 2013.
12. These are rare but verified phenomena, especially reported by Dr. Moody.
13. Second International Medical Conference on Near-Death Experiences, March 9–10, 2013, Marseilles, France.

Third Testimony

1. Eben Alexander, *Proof of Heaven: A Neurosurgeon's Journey into the Afterlife* (New York: Simon & Shuster, 2012).
2. Eben Alexander, "Proof of Heaven: A Doctor's Experience with the Afterlife," *Newsweek,* October 8, 2012, http://www.newsweek.com/proof-heaven-doctors-experience-afterlife-65327.
3. Ibid.
4. Ibid.
5. Ibid.
6. Ibid.

A Scientific Problem

1. This term is used today instead of "cerebral death" to clearly indicate that all neurological functions have ceased, instead of just the functions of the cerebral hemispheres.

2. See Pierre d'Ornellas, chap. 2 in *Bioéthique : propos pour un dialogue* [Bioethics: a proposal for a dialogue] (Paris: Lethielleux, 2009).

3. A PET scan of the brain during cardiac arrest seems to indicate that it still has residual physiological activity (within a certain timeframe) that differentiates it from a "dead brain."

4. Pim van Lommel, "Near-Death Experiences in Survivors of Cardiac Arrest: A Prospective Study in the Netherlands," *Lancet* 358 (December 15, 2001): 2039–45.

5. Sam Parnia authored *What Happens When We Die? A Groundbreaking Study into the Nature of Life and Death* (New York: Hay House, 2006).

6. Emily Kent Smith and Tania Steere, "Have Scientists Proved There Is Life After Death? Research into 'Near-Death' Experiences Reveals Awareness May Continue Even After the Brain Has Shut Down," *Daily Mail*, October 6, 2014, http://www.dailymail.co.uk/health/article-2783030/Research-near-death -experiences-reveals-awareness-continue-brain-shut-down.html.

7. Ibid.

8. Melvin Morse, *La divine connexion* [The divine connection] (Paris: Le Jardin des Livres, 2002), 61, 76–77.

9. Dr. Jean-Pierre Jourdan, from a talk at the California Institute of Technology in June 21, 2015.

10. Proceedings from the First International Medical Conference on Near-Death Experiences, June 17, 2016, in Martigues, France, page 44.

Fourth Testimony

1. From an interview in the monthly magazine *Il est vivant* [He is alive] 314 (April 2014): 26–33.

2. Ibid.

3. Ibid.

4. Ibid.

5. Natalie Saracco did not know of this vision before her accident.

6. See http://www.sanctuaires-paray.com. Retreats and sessions on the Heart of Jesus are held throughout the year in this holy place of Paray-le-Monial.

Religious Approach

1. That is, believing without the help of reasoning. This can also be the case with those who are flooded with miracles or apparitions and who henceforth lean on them as a primary impetus for their faith.

2. Evelyn Elsaesser-Valarino, *On the Other Side of Life: Exploring the Phenomenon of Near-Death Experience* (New York: Da Capo Press, 1997).

3. See in particular François Brune, *Les morts nous parlent* [The dead speak to us], 2 vols. (Paris: Le livre de Poche, 2012).

4. See the end of this chapter.

5. The author here uses the French expression "indices pensables," which translates as "thought-provoking clues" but also is a play on words for the "indispensables."

6. I also discovered on the web that Bishop A. M. Léonard, archbishop of Malines-Bruxelles, had a similar opinion. See http://questions.aleteia.org/.

7. Michel Aupetit, *La mort, et après ?* [Death, and then?] (Paris: Salvator, 2009). Available in French only.

8. According to Abbot Jean-Pascal Perreux, medical doctor and moral theologian, author of *Theologie morale fondamentale* [Fundamental moral theology], 5 vols. (Saint-Cénéré: Téqui, 2008).

9. See the *Catechism of the Catholic Church*, 2nd ed., 1022, accessed July 20, 2016, www.vatican.va/archive/ENG0015/_INDEX.HTM.

Fifth Testimony

1. Interview on Radio-Maria in Columbia, *Dra. Gloria Polo. Testimonio místico. Colombia.*

2. We know that the seers of Fatima had a vision of hell.

3. *The Life of Saint Teresa of Avila by Herself,* Chapter 32.

4. Adapted by translator from the original version of the statement at www.netz.gpo.cc/ to match the author's version. A similar testimony to Gloria Polo's was given by Father James Manjackal, MSFS, in a small booklet of 169 pages titled *J'ai vu l'éternité* [I saw eternity] (Verbum Dei, 2014).

5. Michel Henry, *I Am the Truth; Toward a Philosophy of Christianity* (Redwood City, CA: Stanford University Press, 2002).

6. Michel Aupetit, *L'embryon, quels enjeux ?* [The embryo, at what cost?] (Paris: Salvator, 2008).

Anthropological Approach

1. "I will take away your stubborn heart and give you a new heart and a desire to be faithful" (Ezekiel 36:26).

2. Negentropy and entropy.

3. Aristotle, Greek philosopher (384–322 BC), preceptor of Alexander the Great and disciple of Plato.

4. Claude Tresmontant, *Problèmes de notre temps* [Problems of our time] (O.E.I.L., 1991).

5. "The word 'principle,' synonym of the words 'cause' and 'origin,' comes from the Latin *principium*, which means 'from the beginning, at the origin, that which acts first.' The ultimate principle, the Principle of principles, the Cause of all causes is the living Being itself out of which all arises. This supreme pure spirit absolutely spiritual Being can be called God. It has been so for millennia" (H. Gavignet, *Il n'y a que deux jours* [It's been only two days] [Saint-Cénéré: Tequi, 1981]).

6. Saint Thomas Aquinas says, "the form of the body."

7. Ephrem Yon, *L'homme selon l'Esprit* [Man according to spirit] (Paris: DDB, 1995), an essential book that is unfortunately no longer available.

8. Unfortunately, the term *spirit* has been robbed of its original spiritual meaning and tends to be used in its rational sense.

9. This is not the case with animals, which obviously have a soul because they are alive, but whose soul depends on the very matter to which it is linked. It is therefore corporeal and mortal.

10. Gustave Martelet, *L'au-delà retrouvé* [The afterlife discovered] (Paris: Desclée, 1998).

11. The source of worship of saints' bodies.

12. *Catechism of the Catholic Church* (Paris: Centurion/Cerf/Fleurus-Mame, 1998).

13. Ibid. It is further said that "his distinction does not introduce a duality into the soul."

14. Ibid.

15. Making a distinction does not imply a separation.

16. Through the initiative and direction of Pope Benedict XVI himself. *YouCat: Youth Catechism of the Catholic Church*, trans. Michael J. Miller (San Francisco: Ignatius Press, 2011).

17. Ibid.

18. Bernard Sesboüe, *"La résurrection de Jésus"* [The resurrection of Jesus], in *Croire* [To believe] (Paris: Droguet & Ardent. 1999).

19. Ibid.

20. Ibid., 305.

21. Respectively found in Luke 8:41–42, 49:55; Luke 7:11–17; John 11:1–44.

22. For Lazarus, it was evident from the following statement: "you know that Lazarus has been dead four days, and there will be a bad smell" (John 11:39).

23. Physician, philosopher, and theologian Father Pascal Ide, "Near Death Experiences," in *Dictionnaire des miracles et de l'extraordinaire chrétien* [Dictionary of Christian miracles and extraordinary phenomena], ed. Patrick Sbalchiero (Paris: Fayard, 2002), 567–568.

24. Former chaplain of the Notre-Dame de Montligeon sanctuary, which was founded a century ago in l'Orne, France; it was dedicated to prayer for the dead since its inception.

Sixth Testimony

1. A document that was part of the proceedings toward the canonization of Padre Pio.

Other Extraordinary Phenomena

1. We have seen what needs to be thought about it.

2. René Laurentin, in his introduction to *Dictionnaire des miracles et de l'extraordinaire chrétiens* [Dictionary of Christian miracles and extraordinary phenomena], ed. Patrick Sbalchiero (Paris: Fayard, 2002).

3. Patrick Sbalchiero, ed., *Dictionnaire des miracles et de l'extraordinaire chrétiens* [Dictionary of Christian miracles and extraordinary phenomena] (Paris: Fayard, 2002), 768–769.

4. Ibid.

5. René Laurentin and Henri Joyeux, *Études médicales et scientifiques des apparitions* [Medical and scientific studies of apparitions] (Paris: François-Xavier de Guibert, 1985).

6. Which is part of only fourteen official canonical acknowledgments from the Catholic Church.

7. This is also the case with experiencers, who cannot have NDEs on demand, and seers, who cannot experience apparitions on demand. It is a given!

8. Her beatification record was blocked in Rome in 1960 probably because of the abundance of the "marvelous" in which her life was bathed.

9. Who appeared in front of the cockpit of an airplane pilot in the sky!

10. Patrick Sbalchiero.

11. Carnal heart transpierced much like Jesus's heart was hit by the centurion's spear. The term is borrowed from the Latin *transverberare*, meaning to transpierce, and used in mystical phenomenology.

12. It has since become the Maison Saint-Michel, held by the Fathers of Betharram after the Carmel was closed.

13. A small chapel still exists in the park.

14. Unfortunately, the heart was stolen by a mentally ill person who allegedly threw it in the river Gave de Pau.

15. She ended up seeing the blissful Abbott Louis-Edouard Cestac, who had recently passed away (on March 27, 1868).

16. A must-read on this topic, *Enquête sur les miracles* [Enquiry on miracles] (Montrouge: Éditions du Jubilé, 2015).

17. *Lourdes, des miracles pour notre guérison* [Lourdes, miracles for healing] (Paris: Presses de la Renaissance, 2008).

18. In my book, *Lourdes, des miracles pour notre guérison* [Lourdes, miracles for healing], I offer many examples of such transformations in people who were miraculously healed.

19. In the conference proceedings of the First International Medical Conference on Near-Death Experiences, June 17, 2016, in Martigues, France.

20. In the aforementioned reference.

21. In their dreams, people who are blind from birth cannot see, because they do not understand what it is to see.

Seventh Testimony

1. "Life After Death Experience," *Father Jose Maniyangat Eucharistic and Charismatic Healing Ministry*, accessed July 20, 2016, www.frmaniyangathealingministry.com /Content/viewcontent.aspx?linkid=13.

2. Psalm 22:2; 21:2, Psalm of the Dying in Jewish liturgy.

3. Victor Hugo, "To the Mother of a Dead Child."

4. Joseph Ratzinger, *Principles of Catholic Theology: Building Stones for a Fundamental Theology* (San Francisco: Ignatius Press, 1987).

5. See Joseph Ratzinger, *Introduction to Christianity: Yesterday, Today, and Tomorrow* (San Francisco: Ignatius Press, 2004).

6. Jean-Miguel Garrigues, *À l'heure de notre mort* [At the hour of our death] (Paris: Editions de l'Emmanuel, 1999), 126.
7. Ibid., 147–148.

Conclusion

1. Author of many books on NDEs, including *Where God Lives: The Science of the Paranormal and How Our Brains Are Linked to the Universe* (San Francisco: HarperOne, 2001) and *Closer to the Light: Learning from the Near-Death Experiences of Children* (New York: Ivy Books, 1991).
2. Howard Kainz "What Will We Do in Heaven?" *The Catholic Thing*, June 13, 2013, www.thecatholicthing.org/2013/06/13/what-will-we-do-in-heaven.
3. As is described in the Koran, which predicts a paradise that is described as a place of "limitless happiness" (9:72) and with all the pleasures, a plainly material and nonsupernatural idea of heaven.
4. *Catechism of the Catholic Church*, 2nd ed., 1023, accessed July 27, 2016, www.vatican.va/archive/ccc_css/archive/catechism/p123a12.htm.
5. *Catechism of the Catholic Church*, 2nd ed.,1026, accessed July 27, 2016, www.vatican.va/archive/ccc_css/archive/catechism/p123a12.htm.
6. See www.tedxparis.com/laurent-alexandre and Laurent Alexandre: *La mort de la mort : comment la technomédecine va bouleverser l'humanité* [Death of death: how technomedicine will upstage humanity] (Paris: Jean-Claude Lattès, 2011).
7. In particular Saint Joseph, patron saint of the good death. We must not forget the Chaplet of Divine Mercy that was received by Sister Faustina (Helen Kowalska) from Christ himself, who tells her, "The souls that say this chaplet will be embraced by My mercy during their lifetime and especially at the hour of their death" (Diary 754).
8. Tenderness and prayer are the most important qualities of those watching over the dying person.

Epilogue

1. Having lived in Pau, one can understand how I would be particularly interested in this saint; one can only fall in love with her after discovering who she is.
2. Rarely witnessed in one single person.
3. Amédée Brunot, *Mariam, the Little Arab: Sister Mary of Jesus Crucified (1846–1878)* (Eugene, OR: Carmel of Maria Regina, 1984).
4. Ibid.

Further Reading

Catechism of the Catholic Church

- Article 11: I believe in the resurrection of the body, #988 to 1019.
- Article 12: I believe in life everlasting, #1020 to 1060.

Books on Near-Death Experiences

In French, they are already common. Here are those that I've gathered:

Alexander, Eben, and Raymond Moody. *L'évidence de l'après-vie* [The evidence of the afterlife], with a preface by Jean-Jacques Charbonier. Paris: Guy Trédaniel, 2014.

Allix, Stéphane. *La mort n'est pas une terre étrangère* [Death is not a foreign land]. Paris: Editions Albin Michel, 2011.

Beauregard, Mario, and Denyse O'Leary. *Du cerveau à Dieu* [Brain God]. Paris: Éditions Guy Trédaniel, 2015.

Bromberger, Dominique. *Un aller et retour* [A round trip]. Paris: Robert Laffont, 2004.

Charbonier, Jean-Jacques. *Les 7 bonnes raisons de croire à l'au-delà* [Seven good reasons to believe in the hereafter]. Paris: Aventures Secrète, 2014.

Dudoit, Eric, and Éliane Lheureux. *Ces EMI qui nous soignent* [These EMI who treat us—death experiences]. S17 Production, 2013.

Elsaesser-Valarino, Evelyn. *D'une vie à l'autre* [Two lives]. Paris: Dervy, 1999.

Fustec, Jacques. *Entre épreuve et lumière* [Between ordeal and light]. S17 Production, 2010.

Kübler-Ross, Elisabeth. *La mort est un nouveau soleil* [Death is a new sun]. Paris: Pocket, 2002.

van Lommel, Pim. *Mort ou pas ?* [Dead or not?]. Paris: InterEditions-Inrees, 2012.

Menant, Marc, and Serge Tribolet. *Bien réel le surnaturel* [Real supernatural, and yet …]. Monte Carlo: Éditions Alphée–Jean-Paul Bertrand, 2009.

Moody, Raymond. *La vie après la vie* [Life after life]. Paris: Édition J'ai Lu, 2003.

Morse, Melvin. *Des enfants dans la lumière de l'au-delà* [Children in the light of the beyond]. Paris: Robert Laffont, 1992.

Morisson, Jocelyn. *L'expérience de mort imminente* [The near-death experience]. Paris: La Martinière, 2015.

Ragueneau, Philippe. *L'autre côté de la vie* [The other side of life]. Paris: Pocket, 2001.

Sabom, Michael, and Sarah Kreutzinger. *Souvenirs de la mort* [Memories of death]. Paris: Robert Laffont, 1983.

Christian Books on Death and the Afterlife

36 questions sur l'Au-delà, Numéro spécial de *Il est Vivant,* October 2001.

Aupetit, Michel. *La mort, et après ?* [Death, and then?]. Paris: Salvator, 2009.

Bezançon, Jean-Noël. *On a planté grand-père, Semailles d'Évangile en bord de Marne.* Paris: DDB, 2011.

Bot, Jean-Marc. *L'enfer : affronter le désespoir* [Hell: facing despair]. Paris: Éditions de l'Emmanuel, 2014.

———. *Le paradis : goûter la joie éternelle* [Paradise: taste the eternal joy]. Paris: Éditions de l'Emmanuel, 2014.

———. *Le purgatoire : traverser le feu de l'amour* [Purgatory: cross the fire of love]. Paris: Éditions de l'Emmanuel, 2014.

Civelli, Jean. *La résurrection des morts : et si c'était vrai ?* [The resurrection of the dead : what if it were true?]. Saint-Maurice: Éditions Saint-Augustin, 2001.

Cuchet, Guillaume. *Le purgatoire : Fortune historique et historiographique d'un dogme* [Purgatory]. Paris: Editions Ehess, 2012.

Fourchaud, Thierry. *La mort : témoignages de vies !* [Death: testimonies of life!]. Paris: Collection La Bonne Nouvelle, 2009.

Klaine, Roger. *Aussitôt après la mort : Recherche biblique* [Immediately after death: Bible research]. Paris: Cerf, 2011.

L'au-delà. L'avenir des vivants, Numéro de juillet 2012 de la revue *Christus,* n° 235.

Lelièvre, Hubert. *Je veux mourir vivant* [I want to die living]. Paris: Editions de l'Emmanuel, 2011.

Martelet, Gustave. *L'au-delà retrouvé [The afterlife found].* Paris: Desclée, 1998.

Mathieu-Riedel, Élisabeth. *Ne pleurez pas, la mort n'est pas triste* [Do not cry, death is not sad]. Mame/Criterion, 1997.

Monastic Fraternities of Jerusalem. *La mort n'est pas mortelle* [Death is not mortal]. : *Sources vives* n° 127. April 2006.

Pujos, Nathanael. *Ce qui nous attend après la mort* [What awaits us after death]. Plans-Sur-Bex: Parole et Silence, 2012.

Pralong, Joël. *Dis, Dominique, la mort, c'est comment?* [Say, Dominique, death is how?]. Plans-Sur-Bex: Parole et Silence, 2012.

Espérance et dignité pour les fins de vie. Approches chrétiennes de la mort [The Christian approach to death]. *Catholic Documentation* 109, no. 2498 (October 21, 2012).

Works on the Vital Soul and Ternary Anthropology

Gavignet, Henri. *Il n'y a que deux jours* [There are only two days]. Paris: Téqui, 1981.

Les livres de Claude Tresmontant (la plupart chez F-X de Guibert).

Les livres de Michel Fromaget dont *L'homme tridimensionnel « corps, âme, esprit »,* Albin Michel, 1996.

DVD

Faux départ. Enquête sur les expériences de mort imminente [False start: a survey of near-death experiences], directed by Sonia Barkallah. S17 Production.

Le commun des mortels [The common death: near-death experience], Documentaire - Réalisation Alice Bonneton et Sylvain Sismondi, une coproduction Grand Angle Productions, KTO, BIGLO et Armide Productions, 2011; www.ktotv. com.

CD Audio

Callens, Jean-François (Doudou). *Et après ma mort?* [And after my death?]. Maria Multimedia. 4 CDs.

Maillard, Emmanuel. *Gloria Polo et les dix commandements* [Gloria Polo and the ten commandments]. Maria Multimedia.

————. *Maryam la petite arabe* [Mariam, the little Arab]. Maria Multimedia. 2 CDs.

————. *Série Et si demain, j'allais au Ciel?* Maria Multi Media. 2 CDs.

Internet Sites

www.nderf.org/French: Near Death Experience Research Foundation has the greatest number of NDE stories in the world (more than three thousand, of which seven hundred are in French).

www.s17production.com: Sonia Barkallah's website.

www.issnoe.ch: Swiss Institute for Noetic Sciences (NOESIS Center)

http://www.tvqc.com/2013/12/
la-vie-apres-la-mortdocumentaires-sur-les-experiences-de-morts-imminentes/

With a special mention of Natalie Saracco's testimony:

YouTube : www.youtube.com

KTO: http://www.ktotv.com/videos-chretiennes/emissions/nouveautes/
un-coeur-qui-ecoute-natalie-saracco

About the Publisher

The Crossroad Publishing Company publishes Crossroad and Herder & Herder books. We offer a 200-year global family tradition of books on spiritual living and religious thought. We promote reading as a time-tested discipline for focus and understanding. We help authors shape, clarify, write, and effectively promote their ideas. We select, edit, and distribute books. With our expertise and passion we provide wholesome spiritual nourishment for heart, mind, and soul through the written word.